ELITE SERIES

EDITOR: MARTIN WINDROW

The Armada Campaign 1588

Text by JOHN TINCEY
Colour plates by RICHARD HOOK

OSPREY PUBLISHING LONDON

Published in 1988 by
Osprey Publishing Ltd
Member company of the George Philip Group
12–14 Long Acre, London WC2E 9LP
© Copyright 1988 Osprey Publishing Ltd

Filmset in Great Britain
Printed through Bookbuilders Ltd, Hong Kong

British Library Cataloguing in Publication Data
Tincey, John
  The Armada Campaign, 1588.—
  (Elite series; 15).
  1. Armada, 1588
  I. Title II. Series
  942.05′5   DA360

ISBN 0-85045-821-8

Further Reading:

Below are the key secondary works used for this
book. The bibliography in Boynton will lead to the
full range of sources.

Boynton, L., *The Elizabethan Militia 1558–1638*,
Routledge & Kegan Paul, London 1967.
Cruickshank, G. C., *Elizabeth's Army* (2nd edition),
O.U.P., London 1966.
Lewis, M., *The Spanish Armada*, Batsford, London
1960.
Mattingly, G., *The Defeat of the Spanish Armada*,
Cape, London 1959.
Shute, W., *The Triumphs of Nassau*, London 1613.
Parker, G., *The Army of Flanders and the Spanish Road
1567–1659*, C.U.P., London 1972.
Waters, D., *The Elizabethan Navy and the Armada of
Spain*, National Maritime Museum, Maritime
Monographs and Reports No. 17, London 1975.

Artist's Note

Readers may care to note that the original paintings
from which the colour plates in this book were
prepared are available for private sale. All
reproduction copyright whatsoever is retained by the
publisher. All enquiries should be addressed to:
  Scorpio Gallery
  50 High Street,
  Battle,
  Sussex TN33 0EN
The publishers regret that they can enter into no
correspondence upon this matter.

The Armada Campaign 1588

Introduction

In 1558, by virtue of his marriage to Mary Tudor, Philip II of Spain was also King of England. In that year Mary died and her throne was inherited by her half-sister Elizabeth I who, although raised as a Protestant, might have remained friendly to Catholic Spain. The prospects for Philip to be able to dominate the young queen seemed excellent; and yet 30 years later he was forced to send the greatest sailing fleet the world had ever seen to try to destroy her. How had this reversal of interests come about?

Throughout the period Mary, Queen of Scots provided the counterpoise in the relations between Spain, France and England. As a great-granddaughter of Henry VII she had, in Catholic eyes, a better claim to the English throne than Elizabeth. However, she was also the wife of the French King Francis II. A union between France and England would be disastrous for Spain; so Philip II remained friendly towards Elizabeth. When Francis died in 1560 Mary returned to Scotland, her influence in France at an end. Now she presented a means through which Spain could re-establish its hold over England to the disadvantage of the French. But Mary exasperated her Calvinist subjects, and in 1568 she fled to England—and captivity.

In the same year two incidents occurred which worsened relations between England and Spain. The sea-captain John Hawkins had been successfully encroaching upon the slave trade with the Spanish American colonies; but at the harbour of San Juan de Uloa he was treacherously attacked by the Spanish Plate Fleet, and his surviving ships arrived home in a desperate state. Meanwhile, a fleet carrying bullion to the Spanish Army of Flanders had been driven into Fowey harbour in Cornwall by French privateers. Discovering that the money belonged to Genoese bankers, Elizabeth took over the gold and the loan, causing serious

Philip II of Spain ruled the greatest empire the world had yet seen; but lived the life of a monk in his isolated palace. The sailing of the Armada in 1588 marked the high-point of Philip's power; thereafter, despite further efforts to promote the invasion of England and to subdue the stubborn Dutch, Spain's decline and increasing financial ruin were inexorable. (BBC Hulton Picture Library)

disturbances amongst the unpaid Spanish soldiers in the Low Countries. Philip responded by seizing English ships in Flemish ports; and the hostility between the two governments grew.

In 1572 Elizabeth began to offer the Dutch secret support in their war against their Spanish rulers, and the first 'regiment' of English volunteers crossed the Channel. However, the massacre of French Protestants on St. Bartholomew's Day drove a wedge between England and France, and Elizabeth was forced to placate the Spanish. English support

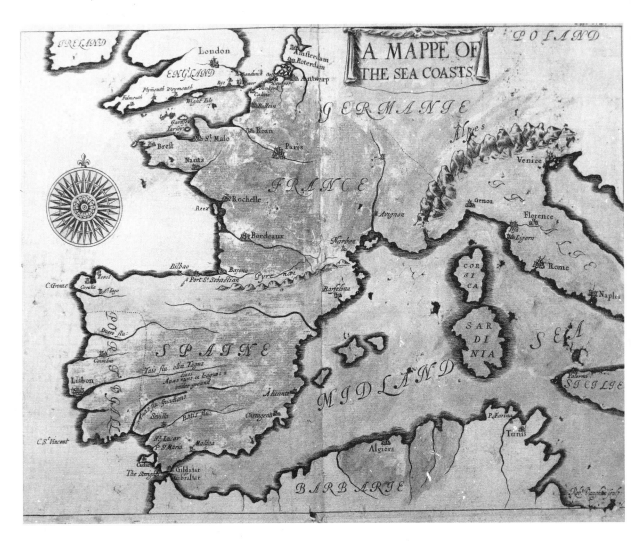

The area of Europe over which Philip II of Spain had achieved political and military precedence. The long-drawn-out Dutch revolt and the increasing incursions of English, French and Dutch traders and sea-raiders into the Spanish-American empire were to lead Spain into desperate and costly efforts to retain her dominance. (K.A.B. Roberts Collection)

for the Dutch continued; and in 1578 and 1580 retaliatory Spanish invasions of Ireland were launched—though both proved disastrous failures. Also in 1580, Francis Drake completed his circumnavigation of the globe and arrived home laden with stolen Spanish treasure.

A major shift in the international balance of power occurred in 1580 when Philip sent his *tercios* to conquer Portugal. At a stroke he gained possession of vast areas in the New World and of a modern Atlantic fleet. The French reacted by attacking Portuguese colonies; but in 1582 Spain's greatest admiral, Santa Cruz, defeated two French fleets at the Azores and at Terceira. To crown his victories Santa Cruz suggested an invasion of England, but the proposed cost was too much even for the Spanish purse.

The assassination of the Dutch leader William of Orange and the fall of Amsterdam to the Army of Flanders forced Elizabeth to despatch an expeditionary force of some 6,000 men to the Low Countries. With English seamen raiding the New World and English soldiers opposing the Army of Flanders, war had been declared in all but name. In February 1587 Mary, Queen of Scots was executed following her involvement in the Babington plot to assassinate Elizabeth. For years advisors had urged Philip of Spain to launch an Armada—a great military expedition—against England; now it seemed that even God called upon him to take revenge. For the heretic Elizabeth, the day of reckoning was at hand.

Spanish Invasion Plans

Philip had been offered two approaches to the problem of invading England. Santa Cruz suggested a self-sufficient naval force comprising 556 ships, including 180 fighting galleons and 40 galleys, manned by 30,000 sailors and carrying an army of 65,000 soldiers; and 200 flat-bottomed landing boats. With provisions for eight months, the total cost was estimated at four million ducats—equal to three and a half years' income from the New World treasure mines. Stunned by the cost, Philip laid the plan aside. In early 1586 the Prince of Parma, the commander of the Spanish Army of Flanders, suggested that with an escort of 25 warships he could ferry 35,000 foot and 500 horse across the Channel in one night. It was an ill-considered boast, and Philip rejected the idea as too dangerous; but it did provide the basis of a plan which would be costly, but not ruinous, and fraught with difficulties rather than being suicidal.

In Philip's plan a fleet from Spain would join with Parma's army and escort it across the Channel. Santa Cruz's estimates could be drastically reduced, as Parma would supply the necessary invasion force, and the Armada would see that the army reached England unmolested. The king made his decision: orders were issued, and the full resources of the Spanish Empire began to grind inexorably towards his objective.

The first plans envisaged the Armada causing a diversion to draw the English fleet away from Parma's chosen landing area. Parma was quick to point out that he had no warships to protect his vulnerable invasion barges, and that even a small English force could destroy them. In a letter of 2 September 1587 Philip outlined his plan to Parma. He estimated that Parma would have 30,000 men available after Ostend had been invested. The Armada would carry 16,000 Spanish infantry, some of them veterans; and of these, 6,000 would be available for operations on land if no naval action was necessary. Santa Cruz would take the Armada to Cape Margate, and Parma's army should be ready to cross the Channel immediately. Once on land Parma could decide on his own strategy, while the Armada might either secure his communications with Flanders, or seize the English ships in their ports. The letter ended with the phrase: 'The obstacles and divisions which may arise (and certainly will do so) next summer, force us to undertake the enterprise this year, or else fail altogether'. This was a chilling observation, given

An impression of the battle of Grave, 1586, in which Queen Elizabeth's favourite, the Earl of Leicester, at the head of English expeditionary troops (right) was defeated by the Spanish. Although at one time Leicester was actually offered the crown of the new Dutch state, his failures in the field damaged his reputation, and led to paralysing disagreements between the English and Dutch which hampered the effort against Spain. (National Army Museum)

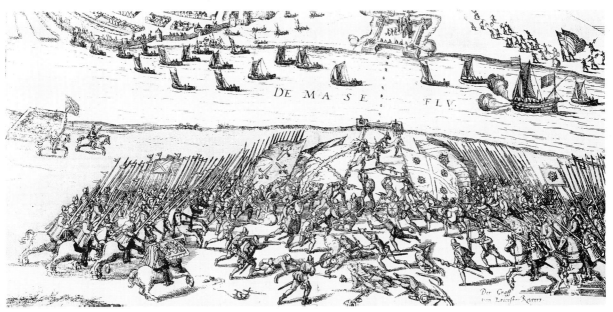

that the Armada would in fact sail 'next summer'.

It is evident that Philip cherished certain illusions about the coming campaign. His confidence in the direct support of God led him to expect good weather even during the winter, when he intended the Armada to sail. The English, who knew the Channel and their own climate, did not man their warning beacons during the winter. It may be that Philip assumed that they would be overawed by the size of his fleet, and took for granted that the Armada would reach Cape Margate in good order and that Parma's small boats would sail unmolested to join them. When the Spanish had fought the French fleet, they had noted that a squadron of English ships had fled as soon as battle was joined. In fact these ships were loaded with supplies, and it was not part of their contracts with the French to get involved in combat. However, the Spanish formed from this incident a poor opinion of English courage, and seem to have expected to find their enemies cowering within the protection of their harbours.

This comforting illusion was shattered by Drake's capture of Cadiz. This daring raid, and Drake's

---

A Contemporary List of the Armada

(From Harleian Mss 168, item 87, f160 & Cal. Spanish Papers f287.)

The Relacon of the Shippinge, municon, victualls and men both soldiers and mariners of the Armie of Spaine, printed in Lisburne and presented to the Kinge the 9 Daye of May 1588.

Imprimus gallions and great Shipps of burden from 600 to 1700 tonnes the nomber is	0065
Item of Hulkes of the Burden from 300 to 700 Tonnes	0025
Item Pataches from 70 to 100 Tonnes are	0019
Item pinnaces of portugalle	0013
Item Galliasses	0004
Item Gallies	0004
The whole number of Shippinge	0130
The whole number of souldiers besides mariners	18,937
Item the mariners	08050
Item voluntarie gentlemen	00124
Item the servants of those gentlemen	00465
Item the gentlemen which serve for paye	0238
Item their servants	0163
Item gonners and theire mates	0167
Item Surgeons and Barbores	0085
Item of friers of various orders to preach	0180
Item gentlemen of the Dukes House	0022
Item their servants	0050
Item Justices to execute Justice	0019
Item in the gallies and Galliasses to Rowe with oares	2088
The whole number of men is	30,655

(The soldiers with the Armada were formed into 7 regiments [six of 25 companies and one of 22, giving a total of 172 companies] under the command of Don Diego de Pimental, Don Francisco de Toledo, Don Alonso de Luzon, Nicolas Isla, Don Agustin Mexia and Gaspar de Sose. The seventh regiment was formed of independent companies.)

Provision of victualls for the fleete for 6 monethes, a quarter and halfe a quarter of Biskett for a man. (*This lists 57,868 Spanish Tonnes of stores including biscuit, wine, bacon, cheese, fish, rice beans, peas, oil, vinegar, leather bottles of wine and water, 5,000 pairs of leather shoes and 11,000 pairs of rope shoes.*)

For the service of the fleets 10 Carvilles 10 small pinnases which have men and goones	00020
The Contents of the Ordinance in the said Army viz 1497 Brasse goones and 934 Iron goones in all	02431
Item shotte for the same	123,790
Item kentalls of powder	005175
Item kentalls of lead for shott	01257
Item kentalls of match	01151

A note of the provision by Land for the Souldiers.

Item Callivers to serve by Land	07000
Item Muskettes to serve by Land	01000
Item Long Pikes	10000
Item Short Pikes	06000
Item Corslettes	10000

More ordinance they have for the desine, besides that which is planed in theire shippes.

Item great Cannons	00012
Item field goones	00021
Item Shott for them	03500
Item Mules to drawe Cannons and field goones into the feild if neede be	0040

The Army of Flanders

Sir Francis Drake, pictured after his circumnavigation of the globe. To the Spaniards 'El Dracque' was a bloody-handed pirate, and a name of terror: they believed that he owned a magic mirror which showed him the position of every ship in the world. His uncanny ability to find prizes was displayed during the Armada fight, when he captured the damaged *Rosario*. Although he was only a vice-admiral in 1588 the Spanish always referred to the English fleet as 'Drake's ships'. (BBC Hulton Picture Library).

The Prince of Parma was the greatest military commander of the age, and the Army of Flanders was considered invincible. The soldiers who made up the army were drawn from many nations, and two different organisational structures were used. The Spanish, Italian, Scots, Irish and English renegade *tercios* consisted of around 12 companies, each with a theoretical strength of 250 men. Each company was made up of either 11 officers, 219 pikemen (half armoured and half unarmoured) and 20 musketeers; or of 11 officers, 224 arquebusiers and 15 musketeers. Two out of every 12 companies in a *tercio* were intended to be shot-armed; therefore a standard 12-company *tercio* would consist of 2,190 pike, 448 arquebusiers and 230 musketeers. The company officers were a captain, accompanied by his page; a lieutenant, an ensign, a sergeant, two drummers, a piper; and a corporal for every 25 men.

German, Burgundian and Walloon foot were organised into regiments of ten companies of 300 men, half shot and half pikemen. (These 'German' companies had two junior sergeants in addition to the establishment of the Spanish company.) The light cavalry, which included both lancers and mounted arquebusiers, was organised into companies of 100 men.

Parma found the preparations for the coming invasion increasingly difficult, with lack of money proving his main problem. A list was drawn up on 29 April 1588 showing the numbers and cost of the Army of Flanders: and the total of 380,421 crowns was impossible to find from the limited resources arriving from Spain. However, it is clear from his own correspondence that Parma had nothing like this number of men available. In March 1588 he wrote to the king that he could find only 17,000 men; while Medina Sidonia was informed that Parma's force would not exceed 17,000 foot and 1,000 light horse, with stores for only two months and only 300 small boats to ship them in. Parma complained that shipments of money and men had been delayed. On 31 January 1588 he wrote to the king:

'. . . both men and money having been delayed beyond the time your Majesty indicated, and

blockade of Spanish coastal traffic, was to disrupt preparations so severely that the sailing of the Armada in the winter of 1587 was cancelled. Another blow came with the death of Santa Cruz—some said of a broken heart caused by the knowledge that the invasion plans were doomed to failure. His successor, the Duke of Medina Sidonia, while not a cowardly fool (as he has often been portrayed), was selected for the authority afforded by his nobility of birth rather than for his military expertise. Nevertheless, preparations moved forward and the Armada took shape. A list of the Armada and its equipment was published and translated into several languages, intended to terrify enemies and impress friends.

particularly the Spanish troops, who are the sinew of the whole business, the numbers, moreover being less than those agreed upon. They have arrived, after all, so dilapidated and maltreated that they do not look in the least fit for effectual service for some time to come. The Italians and Germans have dwindled very much in consequence of having marched so quickly in such bad weather; and in order to keep them near the points of embarkation they are so badly housed that very many are missing.'

The *tercio* of Don Antonio Manrique, 2,000 strong, sent from Castile in 1586, and that of Don Antonio de Zuniga sent in 1587, were both recruited specifically for the invasion of England. Many died during the long, footsore journey from Spain to Holland, and when they arrived Parma described them as 'broken and ill-treated'.

Normal practice in the Spanish service was to place new recruits in garrison in the North African or Italian colonies where they could learn the rudiments of soldiering before going on campaign. The demand for reinforcements caused by the planned invasion led to recruits being sent directly to Flanders, where these innocents apparently passed their free time in dancing and singing as if they were still in Spain. The veterans of the Army of Flanders derisively referred to them as 'the *tercio* of the dance' (*Tercio de la Zarabanda*).

Despite its magnificent fighting reputation the Army of Flanders was not without its problems. The lack of a reliable supply of money with which to pay the soldiers provoked long-running mutinies and prevented Parma from carrying out his military operations. Money was at the heart of the Spanish

Cadiz, the scene of Drake's raid in March 1587, which delayed the sailing of the Armada. His relentless campaign against Spanish coastal shipping played havoc with the logistic preparations for the expedition, and its effects were still felt—in an undramatic but seriously damaging shortage of casks for food and water—during the Armada's voyage to England the followng year. Inset are the Azores, where Santa Cruz gained his great victories over the French in 1582. (K.A.B. Roberts Collection)

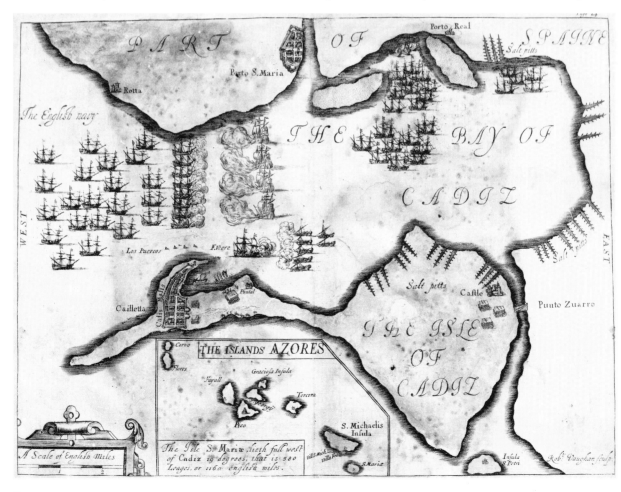

military system, for the ordinary soldier was expected to provide his food, uniform, weapons, and even his ammunition out of his pay. There were many instances where the army was not paid for months or even years, and this led to serious breakdowns in discipline as soldiers straggled off in search of food.

Every year each soldier was supposed to be issued with a cassack (an overcoat), a doublet, breeches, shirt, stockings and shoes. Uniform colours were not adhered to, as individuality in clothing was thought to be essential to inspire soldiers to valour and pride in themselves. The red cross of St. Andrew and a red scarf or sash were worn as identifying marks of the Spanish service. A soldier was expected to buy his weapons, and a cavalryman his mount, by a regular deduction from his wage. With no pay arriving from Spain the soldiers were soon badly dressed and armed, and at times up to a quarter of the cavalry

Combed morion (often mistakenly termed the 'Spanish' morion). Although regarded as old-fashioned, this type of helmet was still extensively used at the time of the Armada. (Wallace Collection, London)

The Army of Flanders, April 1588
(From Spanish State Papers f278)

Statement from the Duke of Parma to the King, showing the Cost of Maintenance for a month of the Army in Flanders, including infantry, cavalry, mercenaries of all nations, artillery, navy, stores, etc; together with a Statement of the Strength of the Forces at the last muster of 29th April 1588:

Spanish Infantry = 8718 men in 89 standards	62,239 Crowns
Italian Infantry = 5339 men in 59 standards	35,225 Crowns
Burgundian, Irish, Scotch Infantry = 3278 men in 29 standards	20,591 Crowns
(The Irish were 918 men under Stanley, the Scotch 804 under Archibald Peyton.)	
Walloon Infantry = 17,825 men in 144 standards	79,341 Crowns
High German Infantry = 11,309 men in 50 standards	86,691 Crowns
Low German Infantry = 8616 men in 34 standards	51,195 Crowns
Light Horse (Italian and Spanish)	38,631 Crowns
Castles:	
Antwerp 600 men, Ghent 350 men, Charlemont 230 men	6,508 Crowns
Staff, unattached, civilians etc. = 668 men	23,204 Crowns
Navy	44,986 Crowns

Summary:	
Army, 59,915 men	380,421 Crowns
His Highness' salary is 3000 gold crowns,	
That of the Maestre de Camps General 1000 gold crowns,	
Commander of the Cavalry 500 gold crowns	5,700 Crowns
Staff and unattached officers	23,204 Crowns
Fleet, ordnance, victuals, headquarters, hospital etc.	44,986 Crowns
Total:	454,311 Crowns

The monthly expenditure up to the present time is 454,311 crowns, equal to 370,000 gold crowns; but this does not include extraordinary expenditure, such as carriers, secret service, spies, travelling expenses, and many other things that are required to be paid for every day. It does not include purchases of powder, and other artillery requirements, or the money which has to be spent when an army is in the field, nor does it include the ordinanry country garrisons.

9

could not find horses. Parma's letters to King Philip constantly return to the lack of money and to the difficulties involved in preparing for the invasion. As early as 5 April 1588 he wrote warning that delays had made the venture infinitely more difficult; and as late as 20 July, the day before the Armada finally set sail, Parma warned that his army might have to abandon the enterprise from lack of supply. 'What account can I give of the fleet, of stores, artillery, and all the rest, unless some resources reach me from somewhere or in some form?'

The true 'Spanish morion' was the most popular helmet of the period; its simple design gave rise to the nickname 'pikeman's pot'. The fact that great princes such as Philip II and Parma chose to be painted wearing helmets like this demonstrates that it was considered fashionable, however simple its appearance. (Wallace Collection, London).

The Nature of War at Sea

Sail versus Oar

The victory of Lepanto in 1571 halted the advance of the Turks and allowed the Spanish Empire to turn to its problems in Northern Europe. Lepanto was a battle between fleets of oar-powered galleys which fought with reinforced rams built into their prows. If an enemy ship could not be destroyed by ramming, it would be disabled and boarded by marines: in effect, a land battle would take place on the decks as the ships became tangled together. The galley had ruled the calm waters of the Mediterranean since ancient times; and although some

vessels had been armed with heavy cannon, these guns fired forwards over the prow of the ship, as the banks of oars and rowers made it impossible to place guns in broadsides.

With the Turks driven onto the defensive and the New World of the Americas becoming increasingly important to the Spanish economy, a new form of naval warfare began to emerge. Sailing vessels armed with broadsides of ship-smashing guns presented new problems to admirals of the galley school, and arguments raged about the relative merits of various ship designs. Early battles between sailing ships had been small-scale affairs, or had been conducted according to the tactical restraints of galley warfare, with boarding and hand-to-hand fighting as the decisive factors. The harsh weather conditions of the Atlantic and North Sea were unsuitable for the low-raked galleys, and they soon began to disappear from the navies of the Western maritime nations. By the time of the Armada only one galley remained in Elizabeth's Royal Navy, and it spent the campaign confined to the safety of the Thames.

The death knell of the Spanish galleys was sounded at Cadiz. Drake's sailing galleons found themselves becalmed within the confines of the harbour, unable to use their speed to avoid the rams of the defending galley fleet. The situation seemed perfect for the galleys as the English ships lay motionless waiting to be smashed in two; but Drake ordered his ships to lower their small boats, and these were able to tow the galleons by bow and stern so that their broadsides could be brought to bear on the approaching galleys. Such was the power of the English guns that the galleys were forced to break off the attack and withdraw to the shelter of the inner harbour. Santa Cruz had wanted 40 galleys to accompany the Armada, but after Cadiz their numbers were cut to only four, and in the event not one of these was able to reach the Channel through the stormy Bay of Biscay.

At a stroke, four-fifths of Spanish sea power had been rendered obsolete. Experienced sailors advised that the invasion should be abandoned; but Philip was determined to continue, and he set to work improvising a fleet of sailing ships. The galleons of the Indies guard were formed into a squadron and, with the Portuguese navy, made up a hard core of 24 purpose-built warships. Forty-one other ships

A 'Spanish morion' of the quality which might be worn by a common solider. It was heavy to wear, but a padding of cloth filled with animal hair or grass would have made it reasonably comfortable. (D. Carter Collection)

were converted to a fighting rôle; and in total the Armada carried 2,431 guns. Thirty-two small ships and 25 cargo hulks completed the fleet.

Oar power was to play a part in the Armada in the shape of the squadron of four galleasses, a type of ship which tried to combine the features of galley and galleon. Although fully rigged with masts and a large spread of sail the galleass also had banks of oars to propel it when the wind fell. Sail power was the normal method of propulsion, so the ship was built like a galleon and had room for a formidable broadside of guns. Much was expected of these costly and well-manned vessels; but although they proved dangerous to the English, their hybrid design made them poor sailers and they were considered a failure.

Ships and Sailing

The key to the English victory in the Armada battles was the superior handling qualities of their ships. The medieval sailing ship had been designed to carry cargo, and was wide-bellied and short in length. This provided the greatest internal storage area for a given amount of shipbuilding materials, but it made for poor manoeuvring and sluggish sailing. The medieval warship was a merchant ship with 'castles' built fore and aft, which proved satisfactory for fighting hand-to-hand engagements. The appearance of ship-borne artillery large enough to damage another vessel opened the way for developments in ship design; and John Hawkins, who joined the Navy Board in 1578, was in the forefront of the new technology.

Hawkins suffered a constant barrage of accusations and allegations from jealous rivals, but even his fiercest critics admitted that the ships built during his period of office were the best they had ever seen. Hawkins realised that naval warfare would be a duel of artillery now that the age of ramming and boarding was over, and he drastically revised the design of the galleon. The fore and aft castles were lowered to make the ship more stable; and, as guns were to be mounted broadside, the hull was made longer and narrower, increasing speed and improving handling and manoeuvrability. Sail design was improved to give the English ships their outstanding ability to sail close into the wind. Such was Hawkins's enthusiasm that of the 24 ships of the Royal Navy at the time of the Armada, half had been constructed to the new principles, and of the remaining dozen, eight had been rebuilt to his specifications.

It is often said that the Spanish ships were larger than those of the English, and it is true that their inferior design gave them higher superstructures; but in fact the English ships were bigger. The Spanish ton was smaller than the English, so that a ship of 1,000 Spanish tons would register only 600 English tons, and in size of fighting ship the English had a great advantage.

Manning levels were very similar in both fleets, for although the Armada contained many soldiers these provided the gun crews which in the English fleet were composed of sailors. Thus in both fleets

Detail from an engraving showing the capture of Isselort by the Dutch in 1588. The Low Countries proved a graveyard for the reputations of Spanish commanders; despite the most professional infantry in the world, and ruthlessly cruel prosecution of the wars against the 'heretic rebels', the Spanish armies were always handicapped by lack of money, and were never able to stamp out Dutch resistance all over the country. Parma was diverted from his re-conquest by orders to capture embarkation ports for the Armada expedition. At top left can be seen officers still carrying swords and bucklers leading calivermen into battle. It is interesting that the Dutch pikemen (right) remain in reserve rather than leading the assault, in the then-conventional manner. (National Army Museum)

roughly one third of the complement of a ship was available to sail her while in action. In terms of gunners the English may have had an advantage, for about one in ten of the crewmen was a 'gunner', which meant that at least every gun in the broadside in action would have a gunner to direct some four seamen in the work of loading and laying the gun. The Spanish lacked experienced gunners, and the opinion of participants in the final battle was that the English were firing two or three times faster than the Spanish.

Guns

In the late 16th century artillery was still in its infancy as a weapon of war. Cannon were costly and difficult to make, and there was little standardisation or quality control. Cannon were graded by the weight of the projectile they fired, and each grade was given a name. However, even this system was not rigidly adhered to, as each authority gave differing classifications to each name. In effect every gun had to have shot made to fit its bore as no two cannon were exactly the same. This was done by passing the shot through a hole in a plank of wood corresponding to the gun's bore:

any shot which was too big was rejected or cut down to size. This resulted in irregular-shaped shot, and in shot which was smaller than the gun's bore; the gap between the ball and the inside of the barrel, the 'windage', prevented the ball travelling in a straight line, thus spoiling the gunner's aim.

Gunpowder also presented a problem, for it was often coarse and unreliable. Not knowing the reliability of his powder, a gunner could not tell how far a given amount would project a shot. Powder was expensive, and there was little opportunity for test-firing or target practice. England had only a small domestic gunpowder industry in 1588, and a shortage of powder was to hinder the English fleet throughout the campaign. The Spanish were well provided with gunpowder, much of it of the fine quality called 'pistol powder', but this may have been a mixed blessing.

The inferiority of Spanish metallurgy showed up in the quality of their ammunition. The fighting ships of the Armada each carried 100 roundshot per

The battle of S'Hertogenbosch, July 1587: Spanish demilancers (centre) defeat Dutch 'Ritter' armed with pistols (low right) and—intriguingly—'Wild Irish' armed with bows (centre right). Note body of Italian and Walloon infantry (top centre) in fixed pike-and-shot formation. (K.A.B. Roberts Collection)

gun as opposed to the 30 per gun held in the lockers of the English galleons. The sudden demand for shot before sailing had caused hurried production, with shot being cooled in water, a process which weakened its structure. Added to the inferior composition of their native iron ore, this made Spanish roundshot prone to distintegration upon being fired, particularly if exposed to the increased pressure involved in the use of high-grade gunpowder. Many of the Spanish guns fired large shot which was expensive to produce in metal, and stone was often used as a substitute. Fired from short-range guns these stone shot would disintegrate into lethal man-killing clouds; but they would have little effect against a ship at long range. English gun foundries were technically far in advance of those in Spain, and new casting techniques allowed the finer, more powerful gunpowder to be used safely. By 1588 the barrel length of the long-range gun, the culverin, was being reduced from 14 to nine feet, but with no loss of range due to the improved powder. The shorter barrel allowed the gun to be pulled inboard more rapidly, and use of the familiar naval truck carriages gave a superior rate of fire over the Spanish, who continued to use adapted field carriages to mount their naval guns.

Philip II had paid close attention to the lessons of Cadiz and to the information his spies brought him of the likely English tactics. Great efforts were made to increase the number of long-range guns carried in the Armada, and Santa Cruz's estimate of 15 per cent was doubled. One reason why the early battles in the Channel were indecisive was that the numbers of long-range culverins in the fleets were nearly equal, the English having 245 and the Spanish 212. It was only with the reinforcement of the English Dover squadron, and the loss of several Spanish ships, that the English achieved a decisive superiority of 330 to 172, and were able to use their advantage to good effect.

Half-armour for a demilancer, with a 'Spanish morion' helmet. The shield would have been carried should the lancer have found himself forced to fight on foot, at a siege or on board ship. (Wallace Collection, London)

The 'Armada Fight'

On 9 May 1588 orders were given for the Armada to set sail from Lisbon to begin its slow progress up the coast of Portugal. The shortcomings of his fleet came as a great disappointment to the Duke of Medina Sidonia, and his disillusionment grew as the days passed. The weather proved unseasonable, and experienced seamen said that they could not remember a May like it. It was not until 30 May that the Armada was clear of Lisbon, and in the next two days only 15 sea miles were covered. After 13 days the Armada had covered only 161 sea miles to reach Cape Finisterre; and it was discovered that much of the food taken aboard at Lisbon had already spoiled and was unfit to eat. Even worse, many ships were reporting that they were short of water, when they should have had sufficient to last for a voyage of two or three months.

The reason behind this logistical disaster lay in the success of Drake's campaign off the Spanish coast in 1587. In addition to the destruction of a large amount of shipping in Cadiz harbour, Drake had waged a less glamorous, but strategically much more important campaign against the small ships plying the coastal trade between Spain and the Armada's base at Lisbon. A large percentage of the cargo that Drake had sunk or burnt had been barrel staves which were intended to contain the food and water to supply the Armada on its long voyage. The loss of this seasoned wood could not easily be made good, and the contractors were forced to make barrels from unseasoned wood. It was these barrels which shrank and split, allowing Medina Sidonia's carefully gathered supplies to rot and seep away.

After a conference of senior officers to discuss the worsening supply situation, the decision was made to put into Corunna, a port on the north-east corner of Spain. Unfortunately the hour was late, and not all the ships had managed to enter the harbour when a storm blew up and scattered those still at sea. It was not until 24 June that the 30 lost ships returned. Medina Sidonia wrote to the king to urge the cancellation of the whole Armada project, citing the large numbers of sick and the shortage of supplies within the fleet. It is clear that the duke had already formed the view that his command would be too weak in numbers and too ill-prepared to carry out the task of invading England: but he received from Philip only a blunt instruction to carry on with the plans as laid down.

When the Armada again put to sea on 21 July the situation had been improved, as repairs had been carried out on the storm-damaged ships and some extra food had been gathered from the surrounding countryside. However, nature had not finished with the Armada and yet another storm scattered the ships. The duke had prepared for this, and by 29 July the fleet had re-formed at its appointed rendezvous. Five ships were missing, including the

A model of the galleon *Elizabeth Jonas* made from the manuscript plans of Matthew Baker. A 900-ton ship of this name figures in the list of the English fleet in 1588; rebuilt in 1597–98, she was listed at 684 tons, but methods of calculation were eccentric. As rebuilt she was 100ft long at the keel, 38ft wide and had a 38-ft depth of hold. Her increased armament comprised two demi-cannon, two cannon-perrier, 18 culverins, ten demi-culverins and ten sakers: a considerable broadside. (Science Museum, London)

Santa Ana of Juan de Martinez, which ran before the storm to La Hogue and stayed there for the rest of the campaign. The *Santa Ana* was the 768-ton (Spanish) flagship of Recalde's Biscayan squadron, and her 32 guns and 300 crew were a considerable loss to the fighting strength of the Armada.

The following day the Spaniards had the Lizard in sight, and a council of war was held to debate whether the main English base at Plymouth should be attacked. Although some spoke in favour of a bold, headlong rush to try to surprise the English fleet and to avenge Cadiz, in the end the unanimous decision was that the Armada should carry on up the Channel to make its appointed rendezvous with the Army of Flanders. The duke reported to the king that the chief arguments put forward were that the entrance to Plymouth was known to be dangerous and well-defended, and that such an attack would be contrary to the king's own instructions. This decision brought much criticism upon the duke when the remnants of the Armada returned to Spain, as it was alleged that his cowardice in failing to attack the enemy at their disadvantage had cost the Armada its best hope of victory.

In fact the decision of the council of war was correct, for on 29 July Captain Thomas Fleming, aboard the *Golden Hind*, had brought news of the Armada's approach back to Plymouth. A screen of small English ships had been positioned to give ample warning of the enemy's approach, and the English fleet was ready to sail at the first opportunity. In the event the ships began to work their way out of harbour at 10 o'clock that night; and as Medina Sidonia and his captains discussed an attack many miles out to sea, a strong force of English warships was ready to meet them anchored off Rame Head outside the confines of Plymouth harbour. On the morning of 30 July the English admiral, Lord Howard of Effingham, led his fleet— which had been made up to 54 sail—out to sea. The English were now well aware that the Armada had arrived, and the chain of beacons blazed along the south coast and inland to London and beyond, so that by the following day towns as far away as York and Durham knew that the Spaniards were at hand.

The first contact between the fleets came on 31 July as the Armada entered 'the Sleeve'. The wind changed to west-north-west and the English manoeuvred to gain the weather gauge of the Armada. Established tactical thinking called for Howard to place his fleet head on to the Armada to block its passage up the Channel. This would have

The Spanish had many of their 'naval' guns mounted on field carriages. They would have been difficult to run inboard for re-loading, and in any one engagement may have been effectively 'one-shot' pieces. (Author's collection)

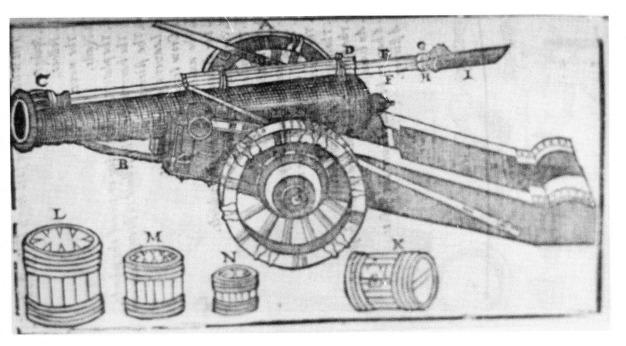

been much to the Spaniards' advantage, for it would have ensured a battle of grappled ships and hand-to-hand fighting, favouring their larger crews and neutralising the English superiority in long-

range firepower. Howard led his fleet around the seaward flank of the Spaniards while another squadron slipped by to landward to join the Lord Admiral. This was a skillful piece of seamanship and

The model of the *Elizabeth Jonas* shows the four-masted rig normal for the larger Elizabethan warships. Main-mizzen and bonaventure-mizzen topsails of the lateen type had now been discarded, and 'square' topsails for these masts (as well as for the main and foremasts) had been introduced, although they are not shown on this model. Both topsails and topgallant-sails were still cut very narrow in the head. (Science Museum, London)

it made a great impression on the Spaniards. However, they replied by executing a 90° turn and moving into a crescent formation with the extended horns pointing backward towards the English.

These first manoeuvres illustrate the difference in the traditions and the approach to tactics of the two fleets. The English were accustomed to fighting in small fleets and in the loose formations called for in Atlantic waters, and they could never have maintained the close-knit formations of the Spanish; but their mastery of the art of sailing in those difficult seas gave them a decisive advantage in ship design and seamanship. The Spanish had been brought up in the long tradition of galley battles in the Mediterranean, where close and careful formation was essential and bad weather seamanship largely irrelevant. There were many fine sailors in the Armada, as the coming days were to prove; but their tactical thinking was hampered both by their lack of experience in northern waters and by the inferior sailing qualities of their ships.

If the Spanish were impressed by the sailing ability and numbers of the English ships, the English were awed by the sheer size of the Armada. Nor was the crescent formation without its tactical subtlety: should the English try to get in front of the Armada, they would lose the advantage of the weather gauge and be swooped on by the Spanish galleons; and if they strayed too close to the rear of the crescent they would be engulfed by superior numbers. This left the option of attacking the protruding horns, where Medina Sidonia had stationed his strongest ships. The Armada's formation thus effectively screened its vulnerable transports while still concentrating the fighting escorts—a neat answer to a difficult tactical problem.

31 July: The First Engagement

At 9 o'clock Howard formed his ships in a single line behind the *Ark Royal*, his flagship, and closed on the southern horn of the Armada, formed by the Levant squadron under De Leiva. Drawing alongside the *Rata Coronada*, the *Ark* sailed across the back of the crescent as the two fleets exchanged broadsides for the first time. The Spaniards tried to close the range, but Howard would not be drawn, and little damage was done. Meanwhile Drake in the *Revenge*, supported by the *Triumph*, the *Victory* and others,

The English captains accepted the appointment of Lord Howard of Effingham as admiral because of his nobility of birth rather than his naval experience; his titular leadership avoided the arguments and jealousy which would have been inevitable among spirited and seasoned commodores such as Hawkins and Frobisher if Drake had been placed in command. Behind Howard in this engraving are scenes from the Armada, and from his attack on Cadiz in 1596. (Author's Collection)

had attacked the northern horn. Here Juan Martinez de Recalde turned his ship, the *San Juan de Portugal*, and waited to be engulfed by the English ships, having ordered the rest of his squadron to remain in formation. The most likely explanation for this strange behaviour is that by offering his ship as bait Recalde hoped to grapple one or more English galleons and so bring about a general mêlée to the Spaniards' advantage. In this he failed; although the English came to within 300 yards and battered his ship for an hour or more, they would not close in for the kill. The issue was settled when the duke sent the Biscayan squadron to the rescue. As the Spanish reinforcements were about to come abreast the English turned and made off. Medina Sidonia formed a line ahead and tried to engage Drake; but the English would not be drawn, and by 1 o'clock the fighting had died out.

At about 4 o'clock the Armada was stricken by two accidents which were to deprive it of two fighting ships. First the *Nuestra Señora del Rosario*, the flagship of Valde's squadron, was involved in a collision and lost her bowsprit. Shortly thereafter Oquendo's *San Salvador* suffered an explosion which demolished her rear section and killed many of her crew. Other ships were appointed to assist, but as the weather worsened the *Rosario* lost her foremast and became unsailable. Reluctantly the duke was forced to take the *San Salvador* in tow, and to order the Armada to sail on, leaving the *Rosario* with her attendants.

During that night Drake was appointed to lead the fleet by the light of his great lantern. Howard lost sight of Drake's light at one point, but then saw it again much further off. He gave chase, and at dawn was surprised to find himself following the light of the Spanish flagship: he was forced to flee hurriedly to avoid being overwhelmed. Drake had in fact put out his light and gone to investigate what he claimed were ships passing near the shore; but

the following morning he came across the *Rosario*, still dead in the water, and at the mere mention of his name the Spaniards surrendered. The richness of the prize seems to have precluded any question of Drake's having abandoned his post from being raised. The same day the *San Salvador* was found to be sinking and was abandoned, to fall prize to Tom Fleming and the *Golden Hind*.

The Manoeuvres of 2–5 August

As the Armada proceeded up the Channel, Medina Sidonia feared that he might be attacked by Seymour's force which had been blockading the straits of Dover. He reorganised his command so that he now led the vanguard and De Leiva the rearguard. On Tuesday 2 August the wind swung around and blew from the east; the Spanish now had the wind gauge, and Howard was determined to regain it. First he tried to pass on the landward side, but was cut off by the duke; then he tacked across to the seaward side, but was countered by De Leiva. Howard then saw that one of his senior captains, Martin Frobisher, was in trouble: he had been caught against the shore of Portland Bill, but the Spaniards were unable to reach him because of

The progress of the Armada up the Channel: note that in the text we follow the 'New Style' calendar, although both styles are shown here. Light winds made for a slow passage, but the weather was better than average for the time of year. Like all sailors of the Mediterranean school, the Spanish liked to keep the coast in sight whenever possible.

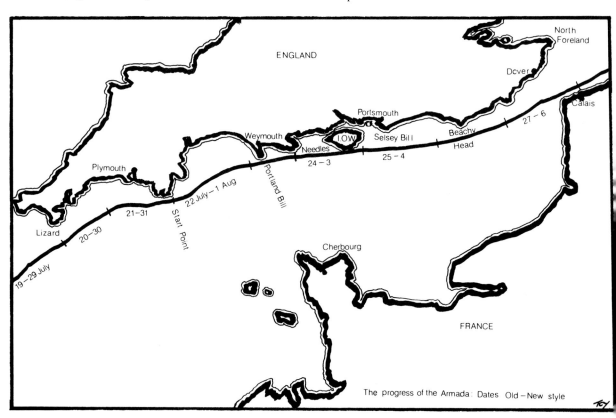

The progress of the Armada: Dates Old – New style

The *Golden Lion*, commanded during the Armada battles by Lord Thomas Howard, was rebuilt to Hawkins's specifications in 1582. She was the same size (500 tons) and carried the same crew (250) and broadly the same main armament (32–35 guns) as Drake's *Revenge*, and the *Non Pareil*, *Vanguard* and *Rainbow*. From an engraving by C.J.Visscher. (Author's collection)

the dangerous tidal race off the Point which threatened to carry them onto the Shambles Bank. Both Howard and Medina Sidonia hurried to the new battle and came to exchange broadsides, but the wind swerved to the west, and Frobisher escaped. By now the English were running short of ammunition, even though coastal towns were sending out in light craft all that they could find. Because of this the fighting on Wednesday was indecisive; and on Thursday there was no wind, so that Hawkins had to have the *Victory* towed by boats to enable him to engage two Spanish stragglers. The oar-powered galleasses soon came up to tow their friends out of danger.

The English had decided to emulate the Spanish, and re-formed their fleet into four divisions commanded by Howard, Drake, Frobisher and Hawkins. When a breeze sprang up three divisions attacked the Spanish rearguard while the fourth was in turn attacked by Medina Sidonia. Frobisher again found himself cut off and to leeward of the enemy, and 11 small boats were sent to tow him out of danger; but a freshening wind enabled him to escape in the nick of time as the Spaniards closed in on him. Meanwhile Drake had attacked the Spanish seaward flank, trying to deprive them of sea room and drive them on to the Owers rocks. Only the skill of the Spanish pilots saved the Armada from destruction, as they turned seaward with only 20 minutes to spare.

By 6 August both admirals faced difficult decisions. Medina Sidonia had received no reply to his messages to the prince of Parma, and without knowing where and when he would meet Parma's invasion flotilla he dared not venture further up the Channel. The lack of a good deep water port, to act as a haven for the Armada should Parma be delayed, had often been raised as a major obstacle to the success of the combined attack on England. The duke now needed that port, and since none could be provided he chose the next best alternative and headed for Calais.

For Howard the prospects seemed almost as bleak, for despite all their efforts and the expenditure of all their ammunition his fleet had been unable to stop the slow progress of the Armada

There are very few contemporary pictures of Elizabethan seamen, apart from portraits of captains. This mariner is from *Habiti Antichi e Moderni* by Cesare Vecelli, published in 1600. Cf. our Plate I; the tall cap, of either fur or fuzzy wool, and the very full breeches—here perhaps tucked up—seem to be common features in the few 16th- and early 17th-century representations of sailors.

or to break its formation. As the Armada neared the coast of Flanders Howard knew that he must take drastic action to destroy or at least disorganise the enemy fleet; and the word went out that in the next action the fighting range must be much reduced. The 35 ships which had been guarding the Dover strait under Seymour's command were called to join the fleet, and more supplies of powder and shot were scraped together from England. Then, as they came to the French coast off Calais, the Armada hove to.

6–8 August: The Fireships of Calais

Before the Spanish ships had taken in their sails the English ships had dropped their anchors, and the two fleets stood eyeing one another under the Calais cliffs. The English were worried that the French would re-arm the Armada, but the Governor of the town would allow only food and water to go to the Spaniards. It was evident to any seaman that the Armada was in a position vulnerable to attack from fireships, and the duke organised a protective screen of small boats to deflect any such attack from their targets. The English now prepared fireships on a scale which befitted the size of the Armada, and eight ships of between 90 and 200 tons were offered by their owners.

The night of 7/8 August found the Spaniards in a nervous state; and soon their worse fears were realised, as eight burning ships in line abreast were carried toward them on the fast-running tide. The outer two fireships were caught by the guard boats and drifted off harmlessly; but as the second pair were approached, their double-shotted cannon were set off by the spreading flames, and the guard boats veered off, fearing more explosions. No Spanish ships were actually set alight, but such was the confusion and terror caused amongst the Armada that ships collided, all formation was lost, and the fleet scattered into the night.

At dawn on the 8th Medina Sidonia found himself with only four other galleons in sight. It was characteristic of the man that he decided to fight a delaying action to give his fleet time to re-assemble. While Howard took his squadron to secure the galleass *San Lorenzo* which had run aground off Calais, Drake led the other three squadrons against Medina Sidonia and his five ships. The weather was now closing in and visibility was becoming worse, so that accounts of the action are localised. Drake raked the Spanish flagship and then led his command off after some other objective, leaving Frobisher and Hawkins to take over the task of surrounding the Spanish ships. Gradually more Spanish ships returned to the fight, until 25 were again forming the remnants of the crescent formation.

The Armada's fighting ships were now desperately short of ammunition, and off Gravelines on 9 August the English found that they could come to close range without suffering serious casualties. On the Spanish ships, for the first time, enemy cannon balls began to smash through beams and splinters sprayed across the decks. Despite the unequal battle the Spaniards fought on heroically, refusing to surrender even when their main guns had fallen silent and they were at the mercy of the English. A sudden squall diverted attention from the fighting

and allowed the Spaniards to break away. Two galleons, the *San Mateo* and the *San Felipe*, were run aground to prevent them sinking, but even in their battered state the Armada shortened sail and offered to do battle again. The English did not accept, for once again they had exhausted their ammunition.

Fate had one last trick to play before the battle in the Channel was over, for on 9 August the Armada found itself being blown helplessly towards the Zeeland sands. The English watched, confident that only a miracle could save their enemies from certain destruction. The *San Martin* drew five fathoms, and the pilot steadily called the depth of water down to six fathoms; everyone was waiting for the sickening jar as they struck the bank, when the wind suddenly shifted and the Armada was able to turn away northward.

In the second week of August 1588 the English

A Dutch engraving of the fireships being sent against the Armada in Calais roads, which owes more to the imagination than to accurate reporting. The Spanish galleys (left foreground) did not reach the Channel; and the fireships were not dismasted before use. There is a clear impression, however, of the lower fore- and after-castles of the English ships (top right) as compared with the Spanish. In terms of overall tonnage and broadside the English warships were not, in fact, inferior to the Spanish galleons, a misinterpretation of the different weights of Spanish and English 'tons' which has passed into legend. (BBC Hulton Picture Library)

viewed the events in the Channel as something a great deal less than a victory, for they firmly believed that the Armada would return; indeed, the Spanish council of war voted to do just that as soon as the wind changed. But the wind remained constant, and the Armada was forced to run before it north and west around Britain, to be wrecked on the coasts of Scotland and Ireland. Only 65 ships returned to Spain, and of those only half were fit to be repaired.

The Ships of Elizabeth's Royal Navy

Name	Built	Tons	Sailors	Gunners	Sold.	Crew	C.	DC.	CU.	DCU.	S.	M.	SP.	Total
Ark	1587	800	270	34	126	430	4	4	12	12	6		17	55
Elizabeth Bonadventure	R1581	600	150	24	76	250	2	2	11	14	4	2	12	47
Rainbow	1586	500	150	24	76	250		8	10	14	2		20	54
Golden Lion	R1582	500	150	24	76	250		4	8	14	9		3	38
White Bear	1563	1,000	300	40	150	490	3	11	7	10			9	40
Vanguard	1586	500	150	24	76	250		8	10	14	2		20	54
Revenge	1577	500	150	24	76	250	2	6	12	2	6	4	11	43
Elizabeth Jonas	1559	900	300	40	150	490	3	6	8	9	9	1	20	56
Victory	R1586	800	270	34	126	430			12	18	9		3	42
Antelope	R1581	400	120	20	30	170			4	13	8		5	30
Triumph	1561	1,100	300	40	160	500	4	3	17	8	6		4	42
Dreadnought	1573	400	130	20	40	190	2		4	11	10		5	32
Mary Rose	1556	600	150	24	76	250		4	11	10	4		7	36
Non Pareil	R1584	500	150	24	76	250	2	3	7	8	12		6	38
Hope	R1584	600	160	25	85	270	2	4	9	11	4	.	18	48
Bonavolia (galley)	1584					250								
Swiftsure	1573	400	120	20	40	180	2		5	12	8		15	42
Swallow	R1573	360	110	20	30	160						2	6	8
Foresight	1570	300	110	20	20	150			14	8	3		12	37
Aid	1562	250	90	16	14	120				8	2	4	4	18
Bull	R1570	200	80	12	8	100								
Tiger	R1570	200	80	12	8	100			4	8	8		10	30
Tremontana	1586	150	55	8	7	70					12	7	2	21
Scout	1577	120	55	8	7	70					4		6	10
Achates	1573	100	45	8	7	60				6		2	5	13
Charles	1586	70	32	6	7	45					8		8	16
Moon	1586	60	30	5	5	40					4	4	1	9
Advice	1586	50	30	5	5	40					4	2	3	9
Merlin	1579	50	26	5	4	35							7	7
Spy	1586	50	30	5	5	40					4	2	3	9
Sun	1586	40	24	4	2	30				1			4	5
Cygnet	1585	30				20						1	2	3
Brygandine	1583	90				35								
George		100				24								

Key: *Sold.* = soldiers; *R* = year rebuilt; *C* = cannon (50lb. shot); *DC* = demi-cannon (32lb. shot); *CU* = culverin (17lb. shot); *DCU* = Demi-Culverin (9lb. shot); *S* = saker (5lb. shot); *M* = minion (4 lb. shot); *SP* = small piece.

The Ships of the Spanish Armada

Armada of Portugal under the Duke of Medina Sidonia:

Name	(Spanish) tons	Guns	Soldiers	Mariners	Total
San Martin (Capitana General)	1,000	48	300	177	477
San Juan (Almiranta General)	1,050	50	321	179	500
San Marcos	790	33	292	117	409
San Felipe	800	40	415	117	532
San Luis	830	38	376	116	492
San Mateo	750	34	277	120	397
Santiago	520	24	300	93	393
Florencia	961	52	400	86	486
San Cristobal	352	20	300	78	378
San Bernardo	352	21	250	81	331
Zabra Augusta	166	13	55	57	112
Zabra Julia	166	14	44	72	116
Total: 12 ships					4,623

Armada of Biscay, under Juan Martinez de Recalde:

Name	tons	Guns	Soldiers	Mariners	Total
Santa Ana (Capitana)	768	30	256	73	329
El Gran Grin (Almiranta)	1,160	28	256	73	329
Santiago	666	25	214	102	316
La Concepcion de Zubelzu	486	16	90	70	160
La Concepcion de Juan del Cano	418	18	164	61	225
La Magdalena	530	18	193	67	260
San Juan	350	21	114	80	194
La Maria Juan	665	24	172	100	272
La Munuela	520	12	125	54	179
Santa Maria de Monte-Mayor	707	18	206	45	251
Patax La Maria de Aguirre	70	6	20	23	43
Patax La Isabela	71	10	20	22	42
Patax de Miguel Suso	36	6	20	26	46
Patax San Esteban	96	6	20	26	46
Total: 14 ships					2,692

Armada of the Galleons of Castille under Diego Flores de Valdes:

Name	tons	Guns	Soldiers	Mariners	Total
San Cristobal	700	36	205	120	325
San Juan Bautista	750	24	207	136	343
San Pedro	530	24	141	131	272
San Juan	530	24	163	113	276
Santiago el Mayor	530	24	210	132	342
San Felipe y Santiago	530	24	151	116	267
La Asuncion	530	24	199	114	313
Nuestra Senora del Barrio	530	24	155	108	263
San Medel y Celedon	530	24	160	101	261
Santa Ana	250	24	91	80	171
Nuestra Senora de Begona	750	24	174	123	297
La Trinidad	872	24	180	122	302
Santa Catalina	882	24	190	159	349
San Juan Bautista	650	24	192	93	285

Name	(Spanish) tons	Guns	Soldiers	Mariners	Total
Patax Nuestra Senora del Socorro	75	24	20	25	45
Patax San Antonio de Padua	75	12	20	46	66
Total: 16 ships					4,177

Aramada of the Ships of Andalusia, under Don Pedro de Valdes:

Name	(Spanish) tons	Guns	Soldiers	Mariners	Total
Nuestra Senora Del Rosario (Capitana)	1,150	46	304	118	422
San Francisco (Almiranta)	915	21	222	56	278
San Juan	810	31	245	89	334
San Juan de Gargarin	569	16	165	56	221
La Concepcion	862	20	185	71	256
Duquesa Santa Ana	900	23	280	77	357
Santa Catalina	730	23	231	77	308
La Trinidad	650	13	192	74	266
Santa Maria del Juncal	730	20	228	80	308
San Bartolome	966	27	240	72	312
Patax Espiritu Santo	?	?	33	10	43
Total: 11 ships					3,105

Armada of Guipuzcoa, under Miguel de Oquendo:

Name	(Spanish) tons	Guns	Soldiers	Mariners	Total
Santa Ana (Capitana)	1,200	47	303	82	385
Nuestra Senora de la Rosa (Almiranta)	945	26	233	64	297
San Salvador	958	25	321	75	396
San Esteban	736	26	196	68	264
Santa Maria	548	20	173	63	236
Santa Barbara	525	12	154	45	199
San Buenaventura	379	21	168	53	221
La Maria San Juan	291	12	110	30	140
Santa Cruz	680	16	156	32	188
Urca Doncella	500	16	156	32	188
Patax La Asuncion	60	9	20	23	43
Patax San Bernabe	69	9	20	23	43
Total: 12 ships					2,600

Armada of Levant Ships, under Martin de Bertendona:

Name	(Spanish) tons	Guns	Soldiers	Mariners	Total
La Regazona (Capitana)	1,249	30	344	80	424
La Lavia (Almiranta)	728	25	203	71	274
La Rata Coronada	820	35	335	84	419
San Juan de Sicilia	800	26	279	63	342
La Trinidad Valencera	1,100	42	281	79	360
La Anunciada	703	24	196	79	275
San Nicolas Prodaneli	834	26	374	81	455
La Juliana	860	32	325	70	395
Santa Maria de Vison	666	18	236	71	307
La Trinidad de Scala	900	22	307	79	386
Total: 10 ships					3,637

Armada of Hulks, under Juan Gomes de Medina:

Name	(Spanish) tons	Guns	Soldiers	Mariners	Total
El Gran Grifon (Capitana)	650	38	243	43	286
San Salvador (Almiranta)	650	24	218	43	261
Perro Marina	200	7	70	24	94

Dutch ideas on weapons drill were far in advance of those of
the conservative Spanish. English captains who had fought in
the Low Countries brought the Dutch innovations back to
England, but it is unlikely that the Trained Bands had the
opportunity to benefit from them by 1588. (Author's collection)

Name	(Spanish) tons	Guns	Soldiers	Mariners	Total
Falcon Blanco Mayor	500	16	161	36	197
Castillo Negro	750	27	239	34	273
Barca de Amburg	600	23	239	25	264
Casa de Paz Grande	650	26	198	27	225
San Pedro Mayor	581	29	213	28	241
El Sanson	500	18	200	31	231
San Pedro Menor	500	18	157	23	180
Barca de Anzique	450	26	200	25	225

Name	(Spanish) tons	Guns	Soldiers	Mariners	Total
Falcon Blanco Menor	300	16	76	27	103
Santo Andres	400	14	150	28	178
Casa de Paz Chica	350	15	162	24	186
Ciervo Volante	400	18	200	22	222
Paloma Blanca	250	12	56	20	76
La Ventura	160	4	58	14	72
Santa Barbara	370	10	70	22	92
Santiago	600	19	56	30	86
David	450	7	50	24	74
El Gato	400	9	40	22	62
Esayas	260	4	30	16	46
San Gabriel	280	4	35	20	55
Total: 23 ships					3,729

Pataches and Zabras, under Don Antonio Hurtado de Mendoza:

Name	(Spanish) tons	Guns	Soldiers	Mariners	Total
Nuestra Senora del Pilar de Zaragoza (Capitina)	300	11	109	51	160
La Caridad (English)	180	12	70	36	106
San Andres (Scots)	150	12	40	29	69
El Cxucifijo	150	8	40	29	69
Nuestra Senora del Puerto	55	8	30	33	63
La Concepcion de Capetillo	70	5	30	42	72
San Jeronimo	64		20	26	46
Nuestra Senora de Gracia	60	10	20	26	46
La Concepcion de Francisco	50	4	20	37	57
La Concepcion de Latero	57	5	20	34	54
Nuestra Senora de Guadalupe	75	6	20	29	49
San Francisco	70		20	42	62
Espiritu Santo	70		20	37	57
Trinidad	75		20	47	67
Nuestra Senora de Castro	?	2		23	23
Santo Andres	?	2		26	26
La Concepcion de Valmaseda	?	2		15	15
La Concepcion de Somanila	?	2		27	27
Santa Catalina	?			31	31
San Juan de Carasa	?			23	23
Asuncion	?			23	23
Total: 22 ships					1,168

Galleasses of Naples, under Don Hugo de Moncada:

Name	(Spanish) tons	Guns	Soldiers	Mariners	Total
San Lorenzo (Capitana)	?	50	262	124	386
Patrona Zuniga	?	50	178	112	290
Girona	?	50	169	120	289
Napolitana	?	50	264	112	376
Total: 4 ships (+ 1,200 rowers)					1,341

Galleys of Portugal, under Don Diego Medrano:

Name	(Spanish) tons	Guns	Soldiers	Mariners	Total
Capitana	?	5		106	
Princesa	?	5		90	
Diana	?	5		94	
Bazana	?	5		72	
Total: 4 ships (+ 888 rowers)				362	

English	Ships	Men	Spanish	Ships	Men
Her Majesty's Ships	34	6,289	Armada of Portugal	12	4,623
Merchant ships under Sir Francis Drake	34	2,394	Armada of Biscay	14	2,692
Ships paid by the City of London	30	2,180	Armada of the Galleons of Castille	16	4,177
Merchant ships under the Lord High			Armada of Andalusia	11	3,105
Admiral:			Armada of Guipuzcoa	12	2,600
For about eight weeks	8	530	Armada of Levant ships	10	3,637
For the whole campaign	10	221	Armada of Hulks	23	3,729
Victuallers	15	810	Patches and Zabras	22	1,168
Coasters under the Lord High Admiral	20	993	Galleasses of Naples (1,200 rowers)	4	2,541
Coasters under Lord Henry Seymour	23	1,090	Galleys of Portugal (888 rowers)	4	1,250
Voluntary ships	23	1,044	*Total:*	*128*	*29,522*
Total:	*197*	*15,551*			

England's Defensive Preparations

Since the beginning of her reign Elizabeth's government had striven to meet the threat of foreign invasion. In the early months of 1587 it became clear that such an invasion would soon be attempted, and preparations to meet it were stepped up. By mid-1588, as the Armada made ready to set sail, the seriousness of the situation had dawned on the county authorities. Their efforts took on an air of desperation as the armour of the militia was cleaned and repaired, and agents were despatched to London to buy weapons to make up deficiencies. Orders were issued to the common people not to rush to the coast to meet the invaders, but to carry away all food and to drive off livestock to an appointed place of refuge. The untrained men of the militia were instructed to keep order and to guard against sabotage by spies and Catholic recusants.

It has been alleged that the Council was slow to react to the invasion threat, and that this was a result of the parsimoniousness of Elizabeth. This view ignores the extreme shortage of funds with which the Crown had to cope at this time. The dislocation of the Antwerp banking system caused by the fall of the city to the Spanish, and a general belief in Europe that Elizabeth was doomed to lose her kingdom, made it impossible for her to raise loans abroad. The cost of maintaining the fleet left very little to be spent on land forces; so the Council intended to call up the county militia at the last possible moment, keeping the forces in readiness but still held back from the camps of the Royal Army where they would come onto the queen's payroll.

The national plan of defence called for a large army raised from the northern counties to defend against any possible invasion from Scotland. This force was also to guard against any Spanish landing north of Harwich. A second force was to be formed from the militias of the so-called 'maritime' counties, which would encounter the Spanish upon their landing and contain them until help arrived. The firing of the coastal beacons would be relayed inland, and a system had been devised whereby certain counties would respond to alarms from various possible landing areas: e.g. a landing at or near Falmouth would have been met by 4,000 men from Cornwall, 4,000 from Devon and 3,000 from Somerset. In the event, these forces tracked the Armada along the south coast and were spectators of its final destruction.

The largest force was to be raised for the protection of 'Her Majestie's person', encompassing the contributions of the nobility, the clergy, the queen's servants and a large force of Trained Bands. It was intended that this force should total some 48,000 men, but due to the delays in calling up its militia components it is unlikely that more than 10,000 were ever gathered. The last force was that intended to encounter the enemy, based at Tilbury and under the command of the Lord Steward, the Earl of Leicester. Its pay records indicate that 16,500 foot and 1,050 horse were gathered at the camp, with more men marching towards it.

The shortage of funds became so great that on 7 August the Council ordered that 21,150 Trained Bandsmen from 16 counties were to return home but remain in constant readiness. Despite these counter-orders, the speed with which these forces could have been called together had the invasion occurred is demonstrated by the efforts of two sets of militiamen from Towcester. The first covered the 60 miles to Tilbury in three days, and the second marched 68 miles in only two days.

The Militia

The advances in military technology made in the early 16th century led to the abandonment of the idea that everyone who was eligible should be called upon to serve in the event of a national emergency. Instead it was envisaged that all citizens would contribute financially to the purchase and maintenance of armour and weapons, but that only a select few would be trained in the modern methods of war.

In 1558, during the reign of Queen Mary, the loss of Calais, England's last Continental possession, led to demands for improvements in the national military system. An act was passed clarifying the obligations of the citizen, and laying down what was expected of him. Under this system a man worth £1,000 a year was required to provide six demilancers, ten light horse, 40 corslets, 40 'almain rivets' or jacks, 40 pikes, 30 longbows, 20 bills, 20 arquebuses and 50 helmets. A man worth only £5 per annum was charged to keep a jack, a bow, a sheaf of arrows, a steel cap or 'scull' and a bill. In the event, the less wealthy were grouped together to provide single items of equipment, so that few were poor enough to escape altogether.

Following the Massacre of St. Bartholomew's Day in 1572 England found herself without a Continental ally, and attention again turned to defence. The Trained Bands were formed in 1573, and each county was required to hold General Musters at which Muster Masters appointed by the Crown would inspect the numbers, equipment and

The officers from Sir Philip Sidney's Horse who attended his funeral in 1587 seem—from this illustration in Lant's Roll—to have worn only the 'peascod' back and breast plates of their battle armour. Their coats seem to have false sleeves hanging from behind the shoulders. (British Library)

training of the Trained Bands. Increasing use was made of the office of a Lord Lieutenant set to oversee the working of the local government of a county. Elizabeth was reluctant to appoint ambitious nobles to positions of such power, but as the threat of war with Spain grew ever stronger the organisation of the county militia came to be increasingly the responsibility of the Lord Lieutenant and his Deputies.

General Musters of the Trained Bands were held on average once every three years, except in times of national emergency when they could be called in successive years. Most General Musters took place over three days, the first and last being allowed for the soldiers to travel to and from the appointed rendezvous. The infrequency of the General Musters, and the fact that they were treated as a social occasion and as a military display, has led some historians to conclude that the militia was largely untrained and militarily ineffective. Dr. Lindsay Boynton in *The Elizabethan Militia* has demonstrated that it was never intended that the Trained Bands would rely on the General Musters for their training. Local gatherings were arranged where corporals, themselves instructed by the Muster Master, would pass on what they had learned to small groups of militiamen; and these meetings might be held monthly, weekly, or—at times of greatest threat—even daily.

Training

At this time military training was in its infancy. Soldiers sent to serve in Ireland or the Low Countries received no formal training, and it was left to their officers, and to experience, to instruct them in the proper use of their weapons. The surviving military books of the period tell us much about the equipment to be carried by various types of soldiers and the duties of officers, but for details of training it was advised that reference be made to some experienced soldier. The Foljambe Papers printed by the Historical Manuscript Commission give a good account of the system adopted by the Privy Council.

A Muster Master was appointed for a small group of counties, and was charged with the instruction of four corporals for every 80 or 100 shot in the Trained Band. He was to instruct these corporals in the use of firearms, and to leave them written instructions so that when they passed on their knowledge to their 20 pupils every group would learn a uniform weapon drill. The place of tuition would be arranged to be conveniently close to the homes of the militiamen. To save money the initial training would be with 'false fires', when gunpowder would be put into the priming pan but not down the gun-barrel: this saved a great deal of gunpowder, yet still accustomed the trainee to the 'flash in the pan' when his gun fired. Next the men would be taught to flash their pans in small volleys of five, ten and 15, to teach them the importance of safe weapon handling when drawn up in close formation. An instruction of 1586 (HMC Foljambe f.89) specifies that the training will take six days and that 3 lb of gunpowder will be allowed for each man. We are told that this will suffice, as the first three days will be '. . . appointed to be only with false fires, to assure their eyes to the use of the harquebus'. Once the men are used to their weapons they are taught to load with ball, and to fire at a target 20ft broad and 16ft high, containing in the centre a 'rondel of boards a yard and a half

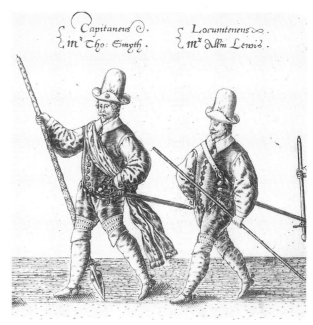

Sidney's corpse was escorted by the 'Cyttizins of London practised in Armes', who fired two volleys over his grave. The officers wore their own clothing even on active service, with jewelled hat pins, taffeta sashes, and lace-trimmed boot-hose to display their wealth. (British Library)

broad, with certain black rondels and a white in the middest'. From a range of 150 paces the soldier is taught to 'level his piece for his better aime and readie discharginge' (SP Eliz CLXXX f.61).

The Muster Master was charged that at least twice a year he should call the Trained Bands together to inspect their weapons and the progress of their training. Those who failed to meet his requirements would be warned to improve their turn-out by the time of the second gathering. These musters were often held on holidays (but not on the Sabbath); and the shot were to be allowed one pound of gunpowder for their training under the Muster Master and for shooting at the mark. The second day was to be spent in 'skirmishing etc.', when the Trained Bands would fight mock battles against one another. When the Council called for a General Muster the Muster Master would find his work inspected by the Deputy Lieutenants of the county, and they in turn were answerable to the Council. In theory the training and equipment of the Trained Bands were subject to rigorous inspection at every level of organisation. Bribery and patronage may have corrupted the system; but as the threat of invasion became increasingly real,

It is recorded that at Sidney's funeral the musketeers wore black 'cassacks' specially made for the occasion. The Trained Bands wore their own clothes when drilling, and were only supplied with uniform when called out for war service. (British Library)

serious training increased. In May 1588 a Spanish spy reported that the London Trained Bands were drilling twice a week, and he judged them to be 'certainly very good troops considering they are recruits, and well armed'.

Weapons

The British Library Harleian Manuscript No. 168 contains a summary of the certificates received from the review of the Trained Bands held in April 1588. From this we can tell with some degree of certainty how every Trained Bandsman in the realm was armed during the coming summer. Before we turn to numbers and proportions we must examine the weapons in use. The standard format requested by the Council included sub-divisions for four categories of arms for foot soldiers: 'shott', 'corslets', bows and bills.

Shott

The shot were sub-divided again into muskets and calivers. There is much confusion over the different types of early firearms, and indeed there was some confusion at the time. We must confine ourselves to the definitions in use in the late 16th century, for terms like 'musket' have changed their meaning and broadened their definitions with the passage of time.

Early in Elizabeth's reign the common firearm was the arquebus, sometimes spelt 'harquebus'. This was usually a matchlock weapon, in which ignition of the gunpowder charge was achieved by a piece of burning match-cord being thrust into the priming pan. The bullet fired was small, but there was little standardisation, and each gunsmith worked to his own ideas of barrel length and weight. This led to the introduction of the caliver, which was in essence an arquebus of a standard bore and barrel length, its name being a corruption of the French word calibre. Knowing that every gun in an army would fire the same size bullet and require a known amount of powder for a given number of shots was a great advantage to a quartermaster.

The caliver became the most common firearm, but experienced soldiers said that the caliver bullet was too small to penetrate armour and was not sufficiently lethal. This gave rise to the musket, a firearm with a longer and heavier barrel, capable of throwing a bullet of two or three times the size of that fired by the caliver. The musket was so heavy that the musketeer needed to use a wooden rest to support the barrel when he came to fire. Sir Roger Williams, a veteran of the Dutch Wars, wrote that although a caliver would fire 20 to 30 bullets to a pound of powder while a musket would only fire eight to 12, the musket was still the better choice because it was more likely to disable its victim. In the more prosperous counties a proportion of muskets had been included in the Trained Bands by the time of the Armada, but the bulk of the shot consisted of calivermen.

In addition to his main weapon, the Trained Bandsman allocated to the shot had to provide all the other items of equipment required for firing and servicing his firearm. He needed a powder flask to store the coarse gunpowder for his main charge, and a smaller 'touch box' to hold the finer priming powder. These flasks were sometimes fitted with two spring-operated cut-off levers so that an amount of powder could be measured into the nozzle of the flask. This gave a reasonably accurate and consistent charge, but soldiers with cheaper

1: English demilancer
2: English light horseman
3: Petronel, Earl of Essex's troops

A

London Trained Bands:
1: Musketeer
2: Halberdier
3: Drummer
4: Caliverman

B

London Trained Bands:
1: Pikeman
2: Fifer
3: Ensign

C

London Trained Bands:
1: Officer
2: Targetier
3: Horseman, Sir Philip Sidney's troop

D

1: Archer, York levies
2: English billman
3: English caliverman
4: English pioneer

E

English Low Countries veterans:
1: Musketeer
2: Caliverman
3: Pikeman

F

1: English caliverman
2: English pikeman
3: English officer

G

1: English ensign
2: English drummer
3: Border Horseman

H

1: English deckhand
2: English master gunner
3: English naval officer

I

1: Spanish musketeer
2: Spanish caliverman
3: Spanish heavy pikeman

J

1: Spanish light pikeman
2: Spanish officer
3: Spanish ensign

K

1: Spanish hargulatier
2: Spanish lancer
3: German Reiter

L

flasks having no measure would have to guess how much powder they were pouring down the barrel. This could lead to an overcharged barrel, likely to explode, or to the bullet falling short when fired from an undercharged gun. One answer to the problem of carrying powder was the 'bandalier of charges'. This was a leather belt from which hung wooden bottle-shaped containers, each holding a measured charge of gunpowder, suspended on strings. The bandalier appears on illustrations of musketeers but rarely on those of calivermen. A mould for making bullets; an iron, or pricker, for clearing a fouled touch hole; and a rammer to force powder, bullet and wadding down the barrel when loading, completed the equipment.

Corslets

The term corslets referred to the pikemen, so named because they wore back and breast plates. The full equipment included a metal helmet, a gorget to protect the neck, a cuirass of back and breast plates, pauldrons to protect the arms, vambraces to protect

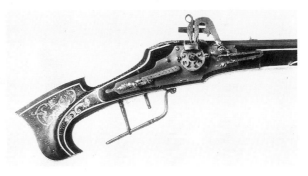

The wheellock petronel was fired with the butt held against the chest rather than the shoulder. It was used in the hope of combining the mobility of the Horse with the firepower of the Foot. (Wallace Collection, London)

the shoulders, tassets to cover the upper thighs and groin, a sword, a dagger, and an 18ft pike. The weight of all this armour would have been a great hinderance to movement, and the expense crippling to the subject who was assessed to provide a corslet for the Trained Band. Both these factors contributed to the gradual disappearance of much of this armour. Troops sent to France in 1589 discarded their vambraces and pauldrons, while the London Trained Bands in 1587 wore only the back and breast plate.

Bows

In the early days of Elizabeth's reign the bow was still looked upon as the greatest strength of England's armed forces. The successes of the bow in the Hundred Years' War were still fresh in the minds of England's soldiers as the last major victories that the nation had won. It was tempting to link the decline of archery with the loss of the Crown's possessions in France, culminating in the humiliating surrender of Calais. Archery was indeed in decline, as is demonstrated by the frequent proclamations instructing both men and boys to practise with bows and arrows suitable to their age. The fact that the government had continuously to re-issue these instructions is clear evidence that they were not obeyed. By 1588 the Council had come to realise that firearms were the weapons of the future, and the use of the bow to equip Trained Bands was discouraged. Orders had already gone out urging counties to convert archers to shot, and in London the bow had disappeared from the Trained Bands, although 20 bows per company remained amongst the untrained men.

Calivermen, marching with arms reversed in the traditional funeral manner. The burning match used to fire the matchlock caliver is clearly shown—centre man, left hand. (British Library)

'Waistcoat' cuirass, opening down the front like a doublet.
(Wallace Collection, London)

However, the debate among military experts raged on; Sir John Smythe, writing the year after the Armada, argued that the bow had a higher rate of fire, was more accurate, was more reliable in bad weather, and produced a fitter, healthier soldier. His opponents replied that a man needed to practise archery from boyhood to be of any use, whereas any weakling could be trained to fire an arquebus in a matter of hours. Since the days of Agincourt armour had been strengthened so that it was proof against arrows. The arrival of firearms which could penetrate the new armour had led to less and less armour being worn, so that an army equipped with bows might well have achieved one success by virtue of surprise; but in the long term the future belonged to the gun.

Bills

The bill was a survival from medieval warfare, and it was only its relative cheapness that allowed it to continue in use for so long. Mounted on a pole of from six to eight feet in length, the bill head combined a diamond-sectioned spike with a curved blade derived from the agricultural billhook. In battle the bill was relegated to a rôle of protecting the ensign, and taking part in the pursuit after victory had been won.

Cavalry

Under the Trained Band system the counties were also required to provide cavalry. Because of the greater expense of equipment for a horseman the numbers involved were always much smaller than those of the foot soldiers, and the system relied on the clergy and nobility to provide the bulk of the armoured cavalry as part of their feudal obligation to the Crown. The horsemen were equipped in three ways: as Demilancers, as Light Horsemen and as Petronels.

Demilancers

The instruction issued to the county of Surrey on 10 May 1586 provides a good description of the Demilancer (Surrey Musters, pp. 320–321, Surrey Record Society 1919):

'A Demylaunce must be furnished with a sufficient stoned horse or large geldinge, a stronge lether harnis, a stell sadle or stronge large bolstred sadle with the furniture therunto: and for the man a Demylaunce harnis furnyshed, a Demylaunce stafe, a sworde and dagger, a cassock of redde clothe garded with twoe gardes of white clothe one ynche broade.'

The demilance was so called because he was originally regarded as a partially equipped 'lance' or knight in full armour. He wore full armour protection for his body, arms and upper legs, but stiff leather boots had replaced his lower leg armour, and he might wear an open-faced helmet rather than a closed helm. Ring mail was often worn under the armour to protect the joints.

Light Horse

The Surrey instruction also describes the light horseman:

'A lighthorseman must have a sufficient geldinge with a stronge sadle and lether harnis furnyshed, the man to be furnyshed with a coate of plate or brygandyne or the Curate of a corslett, sleves with

Chaines of mayle, a northerne stafe, a case of pistolls, sworde & dagger, a Cassock of redde clothe with twoe gardes of white clothe one ynche broade.'

It seems that even the 'light' horseman was weighted down with armour: in 1600 his equipment still consisted of 'Curett, Back, Breast, Collar and headpeece of the best, £01.00s.00d. Pouleons £00.06s.00d. Large elbow gauntletts £00.08s.00d. Petronells with case, flask and mould, £01.04s.00d. Staffe £00.04s.00d. Sword and dagger, wight Turkey £00.13s.04d. Girdle and hangers, £00.02s.06d. total cost £03.16s.10d' (Harleian MSS 3324 f27).

Petronels

The petronel is best described as a carbine with a curved butt designed to be held against the chest when fired. The soldier who used the weapon was a relative newcomer to the English military scene, and his appearance in the muster rolls of the Trained Bands was often because he offered a cheaper alternative to providing a light horseman. It may be that he lacked the armour of the light horse and was regarded as a mounted skirmisher, in some ways the forerunner of the dragoon.

The Muster Certificates

The certificates of the musters of the Trained Bands held throughout England in April 1588 provide us with our best information of the strength and equipment of the queen's forces during the Armada crisis. They must be treated with caution, for not all counties provided all the information requested, and it is not certain that they were entirely honest about their state of readiness. For example, the county of Essex claimed in April to be able to field 4,000 men 'furnished' which is to say fully armed and equipped; but when these men were called to join the army at Tilbury in August the Earl of Leicester was forced to request the supply of '2,000 pikes and 2,000 borgonettes [i.e. helmets]' to supply the Essex men whom he said had arrived unarmed. Despite these reservations the certificates provide valuable information on the quantity, quality and distribution of weapons at the time of the Armada.

The 29 English counties which submitted certificates recorded a total of some 156,500 men able to serve in the Trained Bands. Of these around 85,000 were furnished with arms, and approximately 50,000 had been given some training in their use. The returns provide details of 79,798 weapons held by Trained Bandsmen, comprising 28,742 calivers (36 per cent); 4,702 muskets (six per cent); 21,178 corslets (26 per cent); 14,209 bows (18 per cent); and 10,967 bills (14 per cent). It is surprising, and contrary to some previously expressed opinions, to find firearms forming 42 per cent of the weapons in a survey covering the whole country; and this demonstrates that the militia was not as backward in its military thinking as some have stated. This is balanced by the fact that one third of the Bandsmen were equipped with bows or bills, both of which were considered obsolete. The answer to this contradiction may be that those charged with the organisation of the national militia were up to date in their thinking and knew what weapons were needed, but that the financial

Polearms: left to right: halberd, bill, boar-spear, bill, axe, halberd. (Wallace Collection, London)

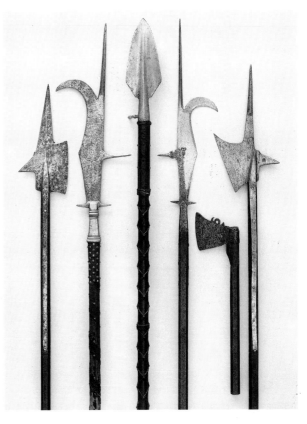

47

The halberdiers do not wear 'cassacks' like the other militiamen in the Lant Roll; each suit has a different pattern of decorative slashings on both doublet and breeches, clearly meant to indicate personal clothing. Their peascod breastplates are apparently of a pattern, however, and may indicate bulk purchase by the company. (British Library)

resources of the ordinary citizen could not always match the demands of the new weaponry.

National figures are of value; but to get a closer picture of the arms of the militia in 1588 we must look at examples of individual counties—for like prosperity and population, the types and proportions of arms used varied from area to area. London provided the best equipped militia. Half of the 20,000 able men were furnished with arms, and of these 6,000 underwent regular training. Each company of 150 men consisted of 60 calivermen, 15 musketeers, 60 corslets, and 15 halbardiers in place of billmen. The 4,000 untrained men were divided into companies of 100 consisting of 30 calivermen, 40 corslets, 20 bows and ten halbardiers. The 50 per cent ratio of shot to polearms in the trained companies compares favourably with Continental practice. The fact that the bows, forming a mere

The Certificate of Kent, April 1588

Ablemen 10,866

Furnished men 7,124 (i.e. those with weapons)

Trained men 2,958:

Officers	Men	Shot	Corslets	Bows	Bill
Sir Henry Palmer					
Edward Boise	850	340	340	170	—
Sir Thomas Scott	300	120	120	60	9
Sir Richard Baker					
John Cobham	600	240	260	100	—
Sir Thomas Fane					
John Loueson					
Thomas Fane	631	252	180	127	72
Justin Campney					
Edward Stile					
Thomas Willoughby	568	220	208	110	30

Total Arms = 2,958 (Shot 1,172, Corslets 1,108, Bows 567, Bills 111)

Untrained men 4,166:

Officers	Men	Shot	Corslets	Bows	Bills
Sir Thomas Palmer					
Henry Crispe					
Edward Crispe					
Erasmus Finche	1,347	454	130	394	36
Sir Thomas Scott					
Sir Richard Baker	1,499	470	292	331	406
John Cobham	570	214	80	101	175
Sir Thomas Fane					
John Loueson					
Thomas Fane	450	180	62	198	10
Justin Campney					
Edward Stile					
Thomas Willoughby	300	40	70	70	120

Total Arms = 4,166 (Shot 1,358, Corslets 514, Bows 1,094, Bills 1,180)

Horsemen:

Demilances, under Sir James Hales	60
Light Horse, under Thomas Palmer	80
Petronells, under Thomas Scott	45
under William Cromer	40
under Roger Twisden	50
under Sampson Leonard	50
Argolets (mounted musketeers) (a Captain for every 60 men)	300
Pioneers	1,077

eight per cent, were all relegated to the untrained companies demonstrates how poorly they were valued. At the other end of the scale comes Oxfordshire, which produced 4,564 able men of whom 1,164 were furnished with weapons. Firearms were carried by 324 men (28 per cent), but bowmen numbered 460 (40 per cent). Lincolnshire and Cornwall both presented almost a third of their militia armed with bows; but overall the gun was in the ascendant, and the Council did its best to encourage the conversion of more archers into shot. The *Instructions given to Capten Shute sent into the Counties of Surrey and Sussex* by the Privy Council on 26 December 1587 stated that he was to:

'. . . cawse the trayned nombers there to be reduced to this proportion of sondrie weapons here set downe, whereof so many to be muskettes as bie anie good perswacion cann be procured. . . . For everie hundreth to be of Shott 50, Pykes 35, Bill 15.'

Capt. Shute's success can be seen from the certificates presented by these counties four months later, as both recorded that 48 per cent of their men were armed with firearms while only nine per cent still carried bows.

We cannot leave our brief survey of the militia without examining the return provided by Kent, the Spaniards' chosen landing place. Of 10,866 able men, 7,124 were armed and 2,958 of these were trained. Of the latter 1,172 were shot, 1,108 corslets, 567 bowmen and 111 billmen. Of the 4,166 untrained men 1,358 were shot (reflecting the popularity of the firearm for 'civilian' uses, i.e. hunting and personal protection); only 514 were the expensive corslets; but 1,094 carried bows and 1,180 bills. Had the Armada landed, these would have been England's first line of defence.

The majority of the militia served on foot, but provision was also made for the raising of militia cavalry. The records of these horsemen are scarcer than those of the foot, but details of 5,461 survive. Light horse accounted for 3,078 men (56 per cent); demilancers 1,049 (19 per cent); petronels 1,034 (19 per cent); and mounted arquebusiers 300 (six per cent). London was not assessed to provide cavalry, but 200 volunteers were offered for the queen's service, although their equipment is not known.

We have already said that the certificates cannot be regarded as totally trustworthy: the counties were bound to put their efforts in the best possible

Serjeants enjoyed higher status than modern NCOs, and wore their own clothing, as did officers. The halberd was a distinguishing feature of their rank; note also the sashes, and pins and scarves on the hats. (British Library)

light. Nevertheless, four months of recruiting and training were available between the time of the musters in April and the advent of the Armada. Officers were despatched by the Privy Council to inspect the preparations of the counties; but in a world where the patronage of great persons such as the Lord Lieutenants was the key to advancement and fortune, it was a brave and foolish man who would report in a direct and critical manner the failings he found. Capt. Thomas Owrde (Howard?) was sent to review the Somerset musters in January 1587, and reported that he had: '. . . founde beyonnde myne expectaton and unto my greate comforte the contrey so excellentlie furnished with all sorts of armour and weapons and that verie good in such p[er]fecte rediness, the men so well sorted and chosen bothe for able bodies and calmye p[er]sonages . . .' (State Papers Elizabeth CXCVII f.50).

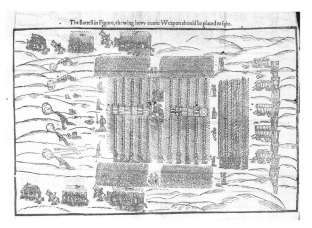

A battle formation from Styward's *Parthwaie to Military Discipline* of 1581, a leading contemporary textbook on military affairs. (British Library)

Of more value is the abstract of the abuses committed by the captains and officers compiled for the Privy Council on 25 August 1588 (State Papers CCXVII f.77). This details not only the incidents of men unpaid for their service and of captains who discharged militiamen in return for bribes, but also lists lost weapons and equipment. Capt. Gardiner's company from Surrey lost eight corslets, nine almain rivets (coats of linked armour plates), five muskets and 25 calivers. Other lost items included swords and daggers, gorgets, headpieces, bills, flasks and touch boxes, corslets, bows, a 'bufierkin' (i.e. a buffskin, a leather jerkin) and several coats. The extent of these losses (given that none were lost in battle and that most men spent only a short period under arms) indicates that the Trained Bands were relatively well equipped, and that the Council was not totally ineffectual in dealing with the abuses of self-seeking officials.

The Feudal Levy

The militia was not England's only armed force in time of national emergency. The nobility and the clergy still owed a duty to raise men to fight in the defence of the Crown, and by this means escaped any liability to serve in or to pay for the militia. The exemption also applied to the servants, tenants and retainers of a nobleman; and the opportunity to escape Trained Band obligations was one of the chief 'perks' of such a position. When the Armada crisis arose the situation was reversed, as noblemen sought to recruit their forces by claiming that certain militiamen owed them a duty as their retainers. Arguments between Lord Lieutenants and local nobility dogged the preparations to meet the invasion.

An abstract of the contributions of the nobility exists in the HMC Foljambe papers (f.164). The total is 1,029 demilancers, 422 light horse, 159 petronels and 1,448 foot; however, the individual contributions of the 26 listed persons vary greatly. The Earl of Essex, a rising favourite at court, offered 180 lances, 65 petronels and 50 foot, while Lord Sandes produced only ten lances or light horse. Sir Francis Walsingham, who was to ruin himself in the queen's service due to his militant Protestant beliefs, raised 50 lances, ten petronel and 200 foot at enormous personal cost.

The list does not reflect all the contributions of the nobility, for a Spanish spy recorded that the Earl of Pembroke (who was not mentioned on the list) accompanied the queen at Tilbury with a retinue of 300 horse and 500 foot. The plans drawn up by the Council made provision for the nobility to raise 16,000 men, but as they did not feature on the government payroll few traces of them remain. Because the Crown did not have to pay the forces of the nobles they were kept in arms a fortnight longer than the county militia drawn to protect the queen. The court officials formed a separate body from the nobility, and their contribution amounted to 612 lances, 350 light horse, 100 petronels and 1,250 foot.

The clergy often proved less than enthusiastic in fulfilling their commitments to the 'Defender of the Faith', but they were ordered to provide 3,883 foot, 21 lances and 538 light horse. A bishop could often provide as many men and arms as a nobleman, but the poorest priests had to be combined so that up to four of them might provide only one equipped fighting man. The clergy fiercely defended their independence from the county authorities, and did not take part in the general musters of the militia or allow the Muster Masters to inspect their contributions. There was some attempt made to produce an organised company on a diocese level, with all of the soldiers wearing a coat of a uniform colour and style.

* * *

Uniforms

During the Hundred Years' War with France a white surcoat decorated with the cross of St. George had become the identifying mark of the English soldier. The Tudor colours were white and green, and white coats remained popular during the first half of the 16th century[1]. When the forces of Sir Thomas Wyatt marched to London to overthrow Queen Mary, both they and the London Trained Bands wore white uniforms, only the mud collected from their long march serving to distinguish the rebels. It has already been noted that the Spanish frowned upon uniformity of dress as bad for a soldier's morale, but the circumstances of English military service led to a more advanced attitude.

Part of the responsibilities of the county authorities was to provide the militia they raised with 'coat and conduct money'. This meant that they issued uniform coats to each draft of men who were called to serve, and paid for their journey, or conducting, to the place where the army was to assemble. As soon as they joined the Royal Army the levies came onto the queen's payroll. The counties had no fixed regulations for outfitting their militia. Troops raised in Essex in 1585 were given

[1]For details see Men-at-Arms 191, *Henry VIII's Army*, Osprey, 1987.

blue coats, but when Essex raised a body of light horse in 1590 they were issued with cassocks in friars' grey with two guards (edging stripes) of blue and yellow. Other counties seem to have stuck to a uniform colour scheme. Soldiers from Yorkshire in 1567 wore coats of light blue with two small laces, red caps and buckskin jerkins. In 1575 Yorkshire light horse wore plate coats, a skull or sallet covered with blue cloth, a blue coat, doublet and hose, and riding boots. In 1587 Yorkshire levies were turned out in cassocks and breeches of blue cloth lined yellow. It is of interest that a description of soldiers raised in Lancaster in 1577 describes the pikemen as wearing 'blue Yorkshire broadcloth', so it may be that blue broadcloth was a particular speciality of that county. The description goes on to note that the pikeman's coat was to be decorated with two stripes of red and yellow broadcloth by way of a border; his vest (doublet) was to be made of white Holmes fustian; his breeches were to be of pale blue kersey with two stripes of red or yellow cloth down the seams, two fingers broad, with garters and points. White kersey stockings and shoes with large

An illustration from Derricke's *Image of Ireland* shows Elizabethan calivermen with left-handed matchlocks; serjeants holding halberds, and wearing burgonet helmets; and mail-clad Border Horse preparing to march; in the background, officers' tents. (British Library)

ties completed the outfit, and his arms were to be a corslet with gorget and headpiece.

Some counties proved to be more generous than others in outfitting their militiamen. The unlucky recruit would be issued with a coat and have to rely upon his own resources to provide the rest of his 'uniform'. Elsewhere considerable pride was taken in giving the county forces a good turn-out, and full outfits were provided.

The term 'coat' raises some difficulty, for it could be used to cover a variety of different garments including cassocks (or cassacks), mandelions (or mandevilles) and galley-gascoines (or gally-gashins). The mandelion was an over-garment which hung loosely from the shoulders; the side seams of the body and the inside seams of the sleeves were not stitched but buttoned together so that it could be worn like a tabard, or with the open sleeves left to hang loose. The gally-gascoine seems to have been a poor man's version of the mandelion, as no buttons were used, the garment being held in place by tapes which tied under the arms. For the common soldier breeches called 'Venetians' (from their supposed place of origin) were becoming the rule. These hung from the waist and reached down to just below the knee, and could be cut to a tight fit or to hang very full. They were much more practical than the enormous *pluderhosen* style of breeches which had previously been worn. Officers also wore Venetians, but the curious 'trunk hose' worn with 'canions' were still in evidence: these gave the effect of baggy breeches from the waist to the upper thigh meeting tight fitting 'shorts' extending down to just above the knee. Much of the equipment must have been produced for the specific occasion when the militia were called upon to serve; but there are indications that the coats were issued to the Trained Bands for their normal musters and collected and returned to a central store afterwards. The Surrey Muster papers (Loseley MSS) record the following payment made on 5 January 1598/9: 'P[ai]d to Seymon th[e] Joyner for making a chest to put the soldiers coates in ij s iiij d'.

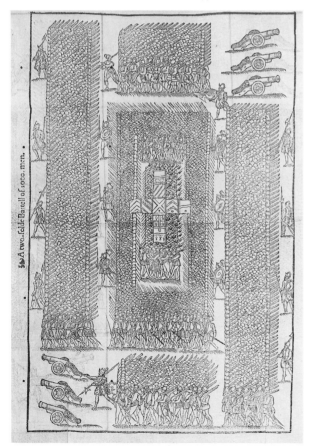

This 'Battell of 2000 men' reflects the way in which military theorists struggled to combine firearms with hand-to-hand weapons. The bills are relegated to defending the colours in the centre of the formation. (British Library)

Could the Armada Have Succeeded?

The invasion of England as envisaged by Philip II was unlike any other military or naval operation that had ever been attempted. For an army sailing in undefended, hardly-seaworthy barges to rendezvous with a fleet operating hundreds of miles from the nearest friendly anchorage would be difficult in itself. To attempt such a meeting in the face of an enemy fleet, particularly when both sides were employing untested weapons and tactics, was sheer folly. Anyone who has been involved with bureaucracy must sympathise with Philip. Trying to co-ordinate preparations over thousands of miles, with poor communications and a financial system always on the brink of bankruptcy, it may be that the only way to get anything done was to brush aside delays and prevarications by ordering that the plan proceed at all costs. Nevertheless, it must be said that there was a stubbornness and arrogance in Philip's nature which made him disregard all

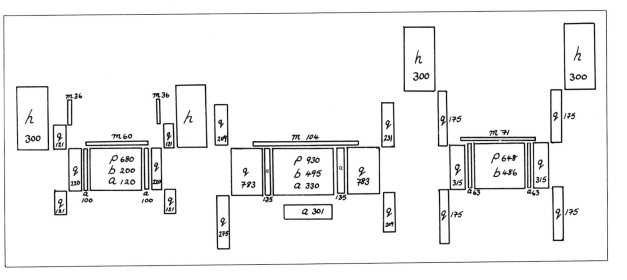

objections to his chosen path. As early as September 1571 he wrote to the Duke of Alva, concerning a proposed invasion of England: 'I am so keen to achieve the consummation of this enterprise, I am so attached to it in my heart, and so convinced that God our Saviour must embrace it as his own cause, that I cannot be dissuaded from putting it into operation'.

It is impossible to say what strategy or tractics the Spanish would have employed had they made a successful landing, for the king left this in the hands of Parma—who made no record of his intentions, and seems not to have believed that the invasion would ever take place. We do know that Parma anticipated having to fight battle after battle before England could be subdued, and that he expected his forces to be dissipated by sieges and garrisons. Even Philip was prepared for less than total victory, for in April 1588 he wrote to Parma to advise him of the minimum Spanish demands should a stalemate be reached and negotiations be entered into. Firstly, English Catholics must be granted freedom of worship; Philip pointed out that the English might reply that he did not give this freedom to Protestants in Flanders, but this could be dismissed by telling them that 'their country is in a different position'. Secondly, all the places held by English garrisons in the Netherlands were to be turned over to Spanish troops. Thirdly, 'an exceedingly great sum' was to be paid to Philip in recompense for all the damage and trouble that the English had caused him. If the whole venture should fail, then consideration should be given to the capture of the Isle of Wight as a bargaining counter and a base for the Armada.

Parma's position would have been unenviable. Lacking a port in which to base itself, the Armada would have been unable to keep communications with Flanders open against the efforts of the English and Dutch fleets. The Spaniards might have been able to live off the land for some time, despite the scorched earth policy advocated by the Privy Council; but they would have found little gunpowder and shot. As increasing numbers of English militia marched into Kent, Parma would have found his bridgehead under a siege that must inevitably have starved him out.

An alternative strategy, and one which Parma would almost certainly have taken, would have been a dash to try to capture London. Remembering that the Spaniards would have needed some time to recover from seasickness and the confusion inevitably resulting from their landing, the question is how quickly could the English have moved the Tilbury and London forces to cover the Medway crossings—the only barrier between the coast and London? Assuming that the planned bridge of boats across the Thames at Tilbury had been completed, this would have presented little problem and Parma would have found his way barred by a strong defensive position.

Although Leicester had shown himself to be no great commander, he was seconded by men of great experience and ability like Norris and Williams, and it is to be hoped that the danger to the nation and the Crown would have caused them to conrrol their quarrelsome natures. As for the common soldiers and people of England, they had been brought up on stories of Spanish cruelties against the Dutch. They had heard how the people of Naarden had been massacred, and that the garrison of Haarlem had been executed despite having surrendered on good terms. They also knew that as a result the people of Leiden had starved rather than surrender to the Spanish; and that the citizens of Oudewater had set their own town on fire rather than let the enemy enter. The people of London knew that 8,000 citizens had been killed and 1,000 houses destroyed when the 'Spanish Fury' had burst upon the great city of Antwerp. With the pamphleteers telling them that the Armada was loaded with Jesuits and instruments of torture, it seemed that the coming battle would be to save not only their Protestant faith, but their very lives.

Historians have often dismissed the military preparations to meet the Armada as a gathering of ill-equipped peasants saved by the Navy from destruction at the hands of a large, all-conquering

The gorget was originally intended to cover the gap between a helmet and breast plate. Surviving much longer than all other items of plate armour, it came to be the symbol of officer status. (Wallace Collection, London)

enemy. The truth is that Parma would have had to fight a brilliant campaign to win final victory, and that one defeat would have caused his total destruction. Since what might have been must remain unknown, we may leave the final assessment of the chances of a successful invasion to Parma himself, in a letter to his king dated 5 April 1588:

'The enemy have been forewarned and acquainted with our plans, and have made all preparations for their defence; so that it is manifest that the enterprise, which at one time was so easy and safe, can only now be carried out with infinitely greater difficulty, and at a much larger expenditure of blood and trouble'.

The Plates

A1: Demilancer

This demilancer represents the heavy 'shock' cavalry of the Tudor army. Horsemen of this type scored a notable success in the skirmish near Zutphen in 1586: although heavily outnumbered by less-armoured Spanish horsemen, English gentlemen volunteers equipped as demilancers held their own, and threw back the previously invincible Spanish cavalry. The increasing use of the musket, which could pierce the thickest armour, and the pike, which could ward off attacking horse, led to the decline and the eventual disappearance of the armoured horseman; but English demilancers played their part in the Dutch victories over the Spanish at Turnhoult and Nieuport as late as 1600. The demilancers would have posed the greatest threat to the invaders' weak cavalry element, which could not have stood against them.

A2: Light horseman

The term is something of a misnomer, as in the hands of an 'armour enthusiast' like Sir John Smythe the light horseman might find himself weighted down with as much plate and mail as a demilancer. Sir Roger Williams, who served in the Spanish as well as the English army, provides us with our best information on many of the weapons and soldiers of the period:

'The seruice of all Light horsmen, consists chieflie in marching of great marches, (Caualgades the strangers term it) I meane, to surprise Companies a

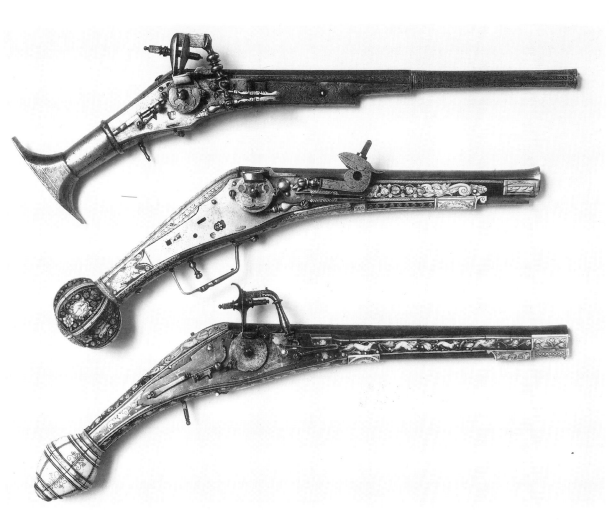

farre off in their lodgings, or marches; likewise to defeat conuoyes, & to conduct conuoyes, as much to say, direct it to spoyle necessaries that come to furnish their enemies, & to conduct necessaries to furnish their own campe or seruice. Also to scout and discouer, to spare armed men, I mean the Launtiers, & the other horsmen; likewise both to conduct & spoile forragers, with the like seruices'.

As the light horseman was more mobile than the demilancer he could harry the flank and rear of an enemy army as it advanced. In battle he would act as support to the charge of the demilancers.

A3: Petronel of the Earl of Essex's troop

As he was a new type of soldier the petronel (or 'hargulatier', as he was sometimes known) was not listed among the Trained Bands, and it was left to Justices of the Peace and others to raise troops voluntarily. This means that descriptions of petronels are difficult to find, and that their

The wheellock pistol was much more expensive than a matchlock weapon, both to purchase and to keep in repair, due to its complex and delicate mechanism; but it could be carried ready cocked, without the dangerous smouldering match of earlier weapons. (Wallace Collection, London)

equipment depended upon the individual who paid for them. As they were principally armed with a firearm they were not expected to come to hand-to-hand contact with the enemy, and were thus less heavily armoured than the light horsemen. A breastplate, a 'jack' of canvas reinforced with metal plates, a brigandine or a helmet may have been their only protection.

Williams argued that the petronel was superior to the light horseman. When attacking an enemy lodging in a village the petronel could dismount and fight just as well as an infantryman. In battle they 'march on both sides of their squadrons, or squadron [i.e. the Lancers] like wings of shot about a squadron of pikes; until the launtiers or curaces charge, diuers of their Hargulatiers march skirmishing before the squadrons . . . when the squadrons charge, they flye on both sides to their fellows . . . they execute more than the Launtiers, after the Launtiers break into the enemies squadrons'.

B, C, D: The London Trained Bands

We are fortunate that the appearance of the Trained Bands was recorded by Thomas Lant in *The Funeral Roll of Sir Philip Sidney* on the occasion in 1587 when they escorted the dead hero to his interment at St Paul's, and fired two volleys over his grave.

B1: Musketeer

The musketeer can be identified by the rest he

Powder flasks were used to carry the main charge of gunpowder for a musket, or to hold finer-corned priming powder in conjunction with a 'bandalier' holding measured main charges. (Wallace Collection London)

carries to support the weight of his weapon. Of every company of 150 men, 15 were armed with muskets and 60 with the lighter 'caliver'. This proportion was high in comparison to the rest of the country, and was in accordance with the best Continental practice. The musketeer wore a 'bandaliers of boxes' to hold his individually measured gunpowder charges.

B2: Halberdier

The halberdiers wore the same defensive armour as the pikemen, and were armed with what was recorded in the muster certificate as a 'bill'. In fact they carried the halberd, a more sophisticated polearm, with a blade for thrusting and an axehead for cutting. The dominance of the pike had led to the decline of the halberd, so that by 1588 only one in ten London militiamen carried this weapon. It was to survive throughout the next century as the distinguishing polearm carried by serjeants and

ceremonial guards such as the 'gentlemen pensioners'.

B3: Drummer

The Lant Roll gives no suggestion that the drummers of the London Trained Bands were more elaborately dressed than their fellow soldiers. The musicians wore the same type of coat, and the distinctive hat with its high-domed crown and small brim. This type of hat was not unique to London or to England, for similar examples occur in Spanish and French pictures during the last quarter of the century. It was sometimes worn with a scarf wrapped around as a hat band, the end trailing at the back of the neck, and with various sizes of brim cocked up in all manner of styles.

B4: Caliverman

Despite the introduction of the musket the caliver remained the standard firearm even in the most modern of the Trained Band companies. A caliver could be purchased for between 12s. and 30s., while a musket cost between 18s. and 40s. A caliverman could fire twice as fast as a musketeer, and each shot would use only half as much gunpowder and lead. These were considerable advantages to anyone who had to equip a Trained Bandsman, and it would be some time before the superior battlefield performance of the musket forced its general acceptance. The calivers of the London Trained Bands are shown as having curved butts in the French manner: this is because they were intended to be held against the chest rather than the shoulder when fired.

C1: Pikeman

The pikemen of the Trained Bands were as much in the forefront of military fashion as their comrades. The Lant Roll depicts them with no protection for arms, shoulders, thighs or knees; even the normal metal headpiece was discarded in favour of the fashionable hat. Their sole defensive equipment, the back and breast plates forming the corslet, was of a 'peascod' design, imitating the fashionable doublet of the same style. The pikemen did not wear the standard coat, for each man had individually decorated sleeves and breeches. No doubt the loose hanging coat would have been difficult to wear

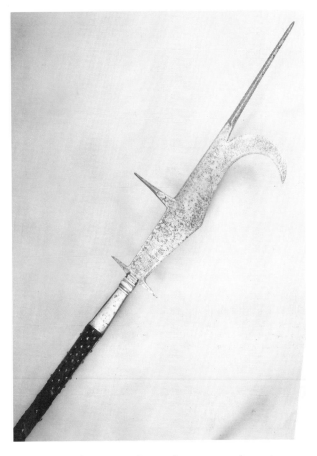

The bill was cheap to produce and easy to use, the customary weapon of the mass of the feudal levy. As soldiers became harder to recruit, however, its ineffectiveness outweighed its economy. (Wallace Collection, London)

under the closely-shaped armour, but cassacks may have been worn over armour on campaign.

C2: Fifer

The fifer dressed like the drummer, but carried a sword suspended from a waist belt worn underneath his coat. His instrument resembled a modern flute more than a fife. Such musicians accompanied the armies to war, but it is not clear whether they had a battlefield rôle like drummers and trumpeters who passed orders by recognised beats and calls.

C3: Ensign

He was the junior officer of a company and in battle was escorted by a guard of halberdiers. At this time most English battle standards contained a cross of St. George as their distinguishing feature. Other devices were red Tudor roses, vertical or diagonal bars, chequers and wavy bars.

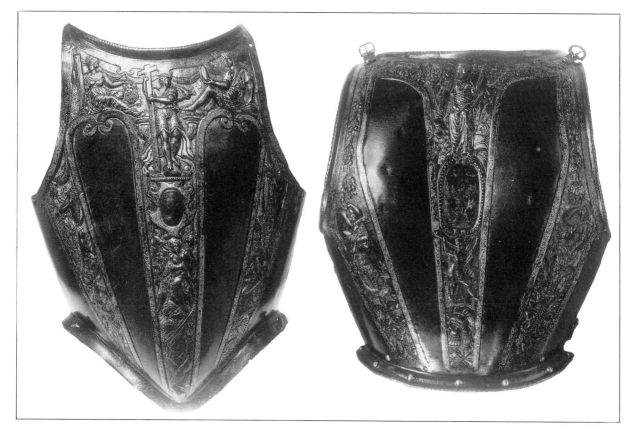

The peascod breast plate emulated the civilian doublet of the day, with its modish protruding belly: a whim of fashion, this added nothing to the strength of the armour. The matching back plate was not as thick, since it was not intended to give protection against bullets. (Wallace Collection, London)

D1: Officer

The officer portrayed in the Lant Roll is Capt. Thomas Smith, a merchant haberdasher who commanded a company from the Bishopsgate ward of the City. As might be expected of a rich merchant, Smith's dress was the height of military and civilian fashion. He wore the same style hat as his soldiers, but the front brim was held back with a jewelled pin. Although his 'doublet' showed a line of large buttons running down the front seam, he wore a 'waistcoat' back and breast plate. Armour made to resemble a doublet was popular, and examples exist in the Wallace Collection in London. His large sash was a symbol of his rank as well as making him easier to identify in the confusion of battle. He wore spurred leather boots reaching up over the knee, but turned back to display the decorative lace of his boot hose. As well as a sword he carried a partizan as a symbol of his captain's rank; its shaft was covered in velvet and fixed with round-headed nails to improve the grip. In front of the captain marched his servant, carrying his shield until the time for battle. By this date the shield, or buckler, was almost obsolete and was carried more for ostentation than for use.

D2: Targetier

Armed only with a sword, dagger and a shield (target), this type of soldier appears only on the certificates of Wiltshire; yet despite their absence from the London certificate, targetiers are shown in the funeral procession of 1587. The shield was often made of metal and intended to be bulletproof. Sir Roger Williams advised that the shield be of light construction:

'Their weights are such, that few men wil endure to carrie them (if they be of good proofe) one houre, I perswade my selfe, the best arming of targeters, is to have the corslets of reasonable proofe, and the targets light; so the bearers may the better and nimbler assaile, and fight the longer in defending'.

It may be that targetiers formed a ceremonial guard, for they still appear amongst the London

Trained Bandsmen carved on the staircase at Cromwell House in 1637.

D3: Horseman of Sir Philip Sidney's troop

The horsemen who appear in the funeral procession represent Sir Philip Sidney's own troop and are therefore not members of the Trained Bands. They wear peascod breast plates over their long coats, but no other armour, and it may be that this was not their 'battlefield' dress.

E1: Archer

A bow was cheaper than a firearm for the individual required to supply a weapon for militia service. This bowman is a poor farmer performing his own service, as he cannot afford a paid substitute. Although he has all the required equipment, much of it is in need of repair. His 'jack' is a coat made up of small iron plates sewn onto canvas—a popular, if rather outdated, form of body armour that was lighter and cheaper than the metal back and breast. In his quiver, eight of the 24 arrows would have had thinner feathers to achieve a longer range: however this advantage was gained only at the expense of accuracy. The uniform colours of his coat are based upon those issued to levies from Yorkshire in 1587.

E2: Billman

The cheapest of all weapons used by the militia was the bill. Often fashioned out of an agricultural or forestry tool, the bill was regarded by many experienced soldiers as useless, and some efforts had been made to have the billmen re-armed with pikes. In 1590 Sir George Carew wrote from Ireland that the best use he had for 'brown bills' was to sell them to farmers of the Dublin Pale. This billman's weapons and equipment would have been handed down to him, and his 'brigandine', a padded doublet reinforced with metal plates and studs, dates from the campaigns of Henry VIII.

E3: Caliverman

The caliver began to replace the hackbut as the standard firearm during the middle years of the 16th century. It had the advantage of being of a standard bore (hence, 'calibre') which made training and ammunition supply much easier. Sir Roger Williams said that a caliver would fire 20 to 30 bullets to a pound of powder while a musket

The burgonet was most popular with horsemen, but was also worn by officers and pikemen. It evolved from the closed helmet of the knight, and gave good protection to the face. (Wallace Collection, London)

would manage only eight to 12. However, he concluded that the caliver bullet was too light, and would not do as much damage as that of the musket.

E4: Pioneer

The government found itself with thousands of able men enrolled in the militia, but with few arms to equip them. One answer was to form pioneer units which could work on fortifying possible landing beaches and chosen places of retreat. They were dressed like the Trained Bandsmen, but their clothing was often made of inferior cloth and they were armed with only a sword and dagger. Shovels, mattocks and axes are mentioned as their equipment.

F1: Musketeer

The figures in this plate represent the English veterans who were recalled from service in the Low Countries to resist the Armada. They are based upon a series of drawings of Dutch soldiers by the artist De Gheyn published in 1587. The musketeer wears an early example of the low-crowned, broad-brimmed hat which was to become almost the standard headgear for musketeers in the next century. He wears a padded doublet under a short cassack with hanging sleeves, and carries a musket rest.

Mail shirts continued to be worn under half-armour even in the 17th century, and are prominent in depictions of troops such as the Border Horse. (Wallace Collection, London)

F2: Caliverman

The caliver continued in service with the Dutch army until 1609, but it is not clear how it and the musket were arranged in battle. In the battle plan drawn up for the English army at Tilbury the musketeers were used as a screen in advance of the pike body, but formed a small percentage of the total of the shot.

F3: Pikeman

This pikeman wears the full equipment of the 'corslet', comprising a combed morion, gorget, peascod breast and back plate, tassets to protect the thigh, pauldrons and vambraces to protect the arms, and metal-faced gauntlets.

G1: Caliverman

The next two plates are taken from *Image of Ireland* by John Derricke, 1581, which depicts the English army on campaign against the Irish rebels. They may be taken to represent militiamen from the maritime counties whose dress and equipment was up to the required standard but not of the most up-to-date style and fashion. The caliverman wears a combed morion, a canvas 'jack' tightly laced across the chest, 'Venetian' breeches, stockings and low shoes. He carries a left-handed caliver, as do all the shot in Derricke's plates. One picture shows these being fired from the left shoulder.

G2: Pikeman

He wears full armour, but with no tassets. His breeches are of the 'trunk hose with canions' style more often worn by officers, and he is obviously better off than the average soldier.

G3: Officer

At this time, and for a century to come, officers did not wear uniform coats even where these had been issued. This officer wears a highly decorated burgonet-style helmet and an impressive but impractical ruff. His breast and back plates are worn over a leather jerkin.

H1: Ensign

This ensign wears the flat cap decorated with a feather that had been fashionable in the time of Henry VIII, but was now outdated. He may be a young or newly-appointed officer, for although his clothes are well decorated, he cannot afford armour other than a gorget. His standard carries the St. George's cross and four Tudor roses, as seen in illustrations of English troops in the Low Countries.

H2: Drummer

He wears a flat-topped, narrow-brimmed hat shaped not unlike a straw boater. His peascod doublet has small shoulder wings, a small stand-up collar and very small skirts below the waist. His breeches are trunk hose with canions, worn with a codpiece.

H3: Border Horse

Drawn from the fierce reivers of the Anglo-Scottish border, these natural warriors served in the army sent to the northern English counties to defend against a possible attack from Scotland. They carried their own weapons, and are depicted clad in long coats of mail and armed with spears and small bucklers.

I1: Deckhand

Taken from the 1588 edition of *The Mariners Mirrour*, this illustration shows that in terms of dress sailors were a race apart. A knitted woollen hat, a long overcoat, and breeches hanging loose to the ankle mark him as a seafarer. His job is to sail his ship while others fight, so he is armed only with a 'kidney' dagger; but like all Elizabethan sailors he is ready to pick up a sword or musket if there is plunder to be had!

I2: Master gunner

A gunner who knew his job was always in demand and his higher status is reflected in his dress. He carries a wooden linstock carved with the head and jaws of a crocodile. The burning match used to fire the guns would be fitted between the jaws, allowing the gun to be fired from a safer distance.

I3: Naval officer

Like their brother officers on land, seagoing gentlemen lived a life far removed from the conditions of the common fighting man. This figure is taken from a portrait of Martin Frobisher, and shows him in typically belligerent mood.

J1: Spanish musketeer

The following illustrations are taken from the works of Theodore de Bry and contemporary engravings. The musketeer wears a plumed morion, a peascod doublet, trunk hose and canions. Around his neck a scarf is tied over his small collar. He is armed with a heavy musket and rest and carries his priming powder in a small flask. His main charges of gunpowder are in wooden bottles or boxes worn on a bandolier. At this time the 'bandalier' was worn over either shoulder, but with the publication of illustrated drill books, notably that of De Gheyn in 1607, it came to be worn over the right shoulder. A drillmaster would also frown on this soldier's habit of holding his burning match in the same hand as he holds his musket: a stray spark could easily set off the priming (despite the pan cover) and fire the weapon accidentally.

J2: Spanish Caliverman

He wears a low-crowned, broad-brimmed hat and a doublet with winged shoulders. His breeches are baggy and tied below the knee with cloth strips. With his ragged and torn clothing, this man probably represents a realistic picture of the state of the Army of Flanders, forced to resort to theft and pillaging to survive.

An engraving from Derricke's *Image of Ireland* shows the Border Horse skirmishing with Irishmen; calivermen fire—from the left shoulder—in the background. (British Library)

J3: Spanish heavy pikeman

The pikemen of a *tercio* were divided between the heavy pike (i.e. armoured) and the light (i.e. unarmoured). This soldier is from the '*tercio* of the dandies' whose clothing was decorated with ribbons and feather plumes. He wears an expensively decorated 'classical' peaked burgonet helmet and has obviously done well from the plunder of the captured Dutch towns.

K1: Spanish light pikeman

This unarmoured pikeman comes from the '*tercio* of the sextons', who were famous for their sombre dress. The light pikemen made up in manoeuvrability what they lost in defensive armour, although it would be another 100 years before all pikemen followed their example.

K2: Spanish officer

A career as a soldier was considered an honourable profession for the younger sons of the Spanish nobility, as a way to find fame and fortune and to restore the prosperity of an impoverished noble house. The Armada in particular offered the prospect of vast English estates which a grateful Philip II would lavish on his victorious com-

manders. This officer wears all that was fashionable for an ambitious officer of the late 1580s. His 'Spanish' morion is of the favoured style, lavishly engraved and well plumed. His peascod breastplate and other armour are highly decorated and well polished. His trunk hose are delicately 'pinked' (in patterns of small cuts and slashes) and his 'canions' are fastened below the knee like breeches.

K3: Spanish ensign

He wears a decorated over-doublet unfastened to reveal his more expensive under-doublet, and has a more comfortable broad-brimmed hat, reserving his helmet for the day of battle. His standard is the ragged red cross of St. Andrew and Burgundy, which was the distinguishing mark of the Spanish forces and which appears in many Dutch engravings of the period.

L1: Spanish hargulatier

The Spanish cavalry were more advanced in the use of firearms than their English counterparts, and the 'shot on horseback' was already an accepted part of the army. The hargulatier combined the rôles of light horseman and petronel in performing skirmishing and patrol duties for the Army of Flanders. In the mainly siege warfare of the Low Countries pitched battles were rare, and the

Derricke's engraving of an Elizabethan general, escorted by Border Horse, riding out to do battle. (British Library)

hargulatiers had little chance to practise fighting in large formations.

L2: Spanish lancer

Spanish lancers appear in Dutch engravings opposing the charges of English and Dutch demilancers, but they existed only in small numbers, for the Spanish found the provision of strong horses just as much a problem as did their enemies. The cassack appears in all the illustrations and may have been the standard battlefield garb, worn over armour.

L3: German mercenary Ritter

These fearsome soldiers in their black armour and armed with a brace of pistols served the English, Dutch, French and Spanish with regard only to their pay. The Spaniard Bernardino de Mendoza in his *Theorique and Practise of Warre* (English

Derricke's idealised picture of an army on the march. In fact Tudor troops in Ireland were usually poorly equipped and badly clothed; sickness was endemic, and there was a good deal of corruption. Life for a soldier marching and counter-marching around the Irish wilderness was harsh, and brutal guerrilla warfare offered little outlet for the romantic ideals of glory and valour promoted by Tudor court culture. (British Library)

translation 1597) says: 'some soldiers of late years would preferr pistoliers . . . with apparent reasons that pistolls were of most advantage for the souldiors, who were easilie caried away with the beliefe therof, in that they found the launce a weapon of much trouble and charge, and the pistoll not so much'.

Sir Roger Williams thought that the pistol, in the hands of a well-trained and determined man, was a better weapon than the lance; but the pistoliers often fired their volley at too great a distance and were charged by the lancers as they turned to retire and reload.

B, C, D L'aspect des *London Trained Bands*, les régiments de la milice anglaise les mieux armés et les plus riches a été noté par Thomas Lant sur ses gravures des unités présentes aux funérailles de Sir Philip Sidney en 1587; et nous nous en servons ici comme témoignage. **B1** Sur une compagnie de 150 hommes, 15 d'entre eux avaient de lourds mousquets. **B2** La hallebarde devenait plus rare par rapport à la pique; un seul homme sur dix en portait une, elle allait bientôt devenir uniquement signe du grade d'officier ou de *serjeant*. **B3** La tenue des tambours n'était pas plus recherchée que celle des autres soldats qui portaient tous leurs vêtements personnels. **B4** L'arme appelée *caliver*, moins coûteuse et plus légère que le mousquet, avait une moindre force de pénétration. On la posait contre la poitrine et non pas sur l'épaule pour tirer. Sur chacune des compagnies de 150 hommes, 60 d'entre eux avaient des *calivers*.

C1 Les seules armures portées étaient celles nommées *peascod*, façonnées avec l'estomac en saillie. **C2** On ne sait pas si les joueurs de fifre qui accompagnaient certainement leurs camarades sur le champ de bataille, y jouaient les signaux donnés comme les tambours et les trompettes. **C3** La plupart des drapeaux de compagnie portaient comme emblème la croix de Saint Georges, avec les roses des Tudors, des raies verticales ou diagonales ou des emblèmes de 'flamme' ondulée.

D1 Les marques sur la *pertuisane* indiquent le grade d'officier—de même que son costume plus riche. Les cuirasses faites pour ressembler à des pourpoints boutonnés étaient très populaires. Son serviteur le précède en portant son bouclier, mais peut-être est-ce plus une marque de rang qu'un équipement sérieux de combat. **D2** Les soldats armés d'une épée et d'un bouclier étaient peu nombreux à cette date; le bouclier était en métal et devait servir de protection contre les balles. **D3** La troupe de cavalerie de Sir Philip a pris part à ses funérailles, ainsi que les *Trained Bands*, Ce costume qui comporte peu d'armure n'est certainement pas représentatif de l'aspect courant sur les champs de bataille.

E1 Les soldats de la milice les plus pauvres, venus des zones rurales, portaient encore des arcs. Celui-ci a pour toute protection une jaque (*jack*) de toile et de petits écus de fer. Les couleurs des vêtements sont celles qui ont été enregistrées lors des levées de troupes du Yorkshire. **E2** La hallebarde était l'arme la moins chère de toutes, elle n'était vraiment qu'un peu plus sophistiquée qu'un outil agricole. La veste qui protège la *brigandine* est aussi très désuète. **E3** Le *caliver* bien que moins puissant que le *hackbut* avait l'avantage d'avoir un calibre standard, ce à quoi il doit son nom—et convenait aux distributions de masse faites aux hommes de la milice. **E4** Il y avait plus d'enrôlés dans la milice que d'armes à leur disposition, c'est pourquoi ils ont été nombreux à servir de pionniers pour fortifier les zones menacées par l'ennemi.

F Vétérans des expéditions anglaises aux Pays-Bas, cette reproduction est fondée sur des croquis de De Gheyn.

G, H Les personnages sont des reproductions basées sur des gravures de soldats anglais en Irlande du livre *Image of Ireland* par M. Derricke, qui a été publié en 1587. **G1** Il porte un *morion*, une jaque (*jack*) de toile et des hauts-de-chausse dits 'vénitiens' ainsi qu'un *caliver* à la main gauche—comme tous les *calivermen* peints par Derricke. **G2** Armure complète mais sans braconnière; le haut-de-chausse est dit 'à canons' (*trunk hose with canions*) et implique un certain grade ou statut. **G3** Les officiers ne portaient pas ces manteaux de couleur uniforme même quand ils étaient distribués aux hommes.

H1 Le chapeau plat (flat hat) est plutôt désuet; et ce jeune officier n'a peut-être pas pu s'offrir d'autre armure que ce *gorgerin*. L'étendard a pour emblème la rose des Tudors à chaque coin de la croix. **H2** Notez le *peascod* et le haut-de-chausse à canons, porté avec une braguette. **H3** Ces cavaliers, redoutés le long des frontières anglo-écossaises, avaient une chemise de mailles en guise de protection, ils portaient des lances, de petits boucliers ainsi que leurs armes personnelles.

I1 Tous les tableaux contemporains de marins les présentent vêtus de bonnets de laine grossiers, de longues capes et de culottes très larges; ce marin est une reproduction d'après *The Marineers Mirror*, un livre datant de 1588. **I2** Son rang plus élevé de canonnier est marqué par son costume, mais notez à nouveau les culottes très amples. Il tient une bouteffeu sculpté garni d'une mèche à combustion lente pour mettre feu aux canons. **I3** Un contemporain belligérant de Drake, d'après un portrait du Capitaine Martin Frobisher.

J1 Ce cliché, ainsi que les suivants, est fondé sur les oeuvres de Theodor de Buy et des gravures contemporaines. **J2** L'armée des Flandres était une bande plus ou moins en guenilles, sans solde et forcée de piller pour se nourrir. **J3** Les piquiers d'un *tercio* étaient divisés en hommes lourdement cuirassés et en soldats sans armure, plus légers. Ce soldat sert dans le 'tercio dit des Dandies', avec en effet des vêtements de style flamboyant.

K1 Ce piquier léger sert dans le *Tercio des Sextons* aux vêtements plus sévères. **K2** Pour le plus jeune fils d'un gentilhomme, s'engager dans la carrière militaire, s'il était ambitieux, était une voie honorable; le costume et l'équipement reflétaient la fortune personnelle. **K3** Un vêtement protège son pourpoint plus onéreux; il porte un chapeau pour plus de confort en dehors du champ de bataille. De nombreuses unités espagnoles aux Pays-Bas arboraient comme emblème la Croix de Bourgogne sur leur étendard.

L1 La cavalerie espagnole, en avance en matière d'armes à feu sur les Anglais, avait plusieurs troupes comme celles-ci; du côté des Anglais, les *hargulatiers* jouaient aussi le rôle de cavalerie légère avec leurs *light horse* et *petronels*. **L2** Le nombre des chevaux appropriés étant insuffisant, la cavalerie lourde espagnole s'en trouvait limitée. Le *cassack* apparaît sur toutes les illustrations et se portait peut-être au-dessus de l'armure lors des batailles. **L3** Ces pistoliers vêtus d'une armure noire ont servi comme mercenaires dans les armées anglaise, française, espagnole et hollandaise, sans plus de distinction.

B, C, D Das Äussere der 'London Trained Bands', der reichsten und am besten bewaffneten englischen Milizregimenter, wurde in Thomas Lants Stichen von Einheiten bei Sir Philip Sidneys Begräbnis (1587) festgehalten; diese Tafeln basieren auf Lants Zeugnissen. **B1** Fünfzehn Mitglieder der 150-köpfigen Kompanien trugen schwere Musketen. **B2** Die Hellebarde nahm im Vergleich zur Pike zahlenmässig immer mehr ab; nur einer von zehn Männern trug sie, und bald war sie lediglich das Zeichen für den Offiziers- oder Sergeantenstatus. **B3** Trommler waren nicht aufwendiger angezogen als gemeine Soldaten, die ihre eigenen Kleidungstücke trugen. **B4** Der Caliver, biller und leichter als eine Muskete, hatte auch eine geringere Durchschlagskraft. Die Waffe ruhte beim Abfeuern an der Brust, nicht an der Schulter. Sechzig von 150 Männern trugen Calivers.

C1 'Peascod'-Kürasse, mit dem modischen vorstehenden Bauch geformt, waren die einzige Panzerung. **C2** Es ist nicht bekannt, ob die Pfeifer, die ihre Kameraden in die Schlacht begleiteten, ähnliche Signale spielten wie die Trommler und Trompeter. **C3** Die meisten Fahnen der Kompanie trugen das Georgskreuz, Tudor-Rosen, Senkrecht- oder Querstreifen oder gewellte Flammenabzeichen.

D1 Der 'partizan' bezeichnet den Offiziersstatus, ebenso wie die reichere Kleidung. Kürasse, die zugeknöpften Jacken aussahen, waren sehr populär. Sein Diener marschierte ihm voraus, mit einem kleinen Schild, vielleicht mehr als Statussymbol denn zum Schutz in der Schlacht. **D2** Es gab nur wenige Schwert- und Schildträger zu diesem Zeitpunkt; der Schild war aus Metall und sollte kugelsicher sein. **D3** Sir Philips Reiter nahmen an seinem Begräbnis teil, ebenso wie die 'Trained Bands'. Diese Bekleidung, mit nur wenig Panzerung, ist wahrscheinlich nicht identisch mit ihrer Schlachtausrüstung.

E1 Die ärmeren Angehörigen der Miliz aus ländlichen Gegenden trugen nach wie vor Bogen. Ihr einziger Schutz war die Jacke aus Segeltuch ('jack') mit kleinen Eisenplatten. Die hier gewählten Farben wurden von den in Yorkshire ausgehobenen Einheiten getragen. **E2** Die billigste aller Waffen war die 'bill', eine Art landwirtschaftliches Werkzeug. Die Schutzjacke ('brigandine') ist ebenfalls sehr altmodisch. **E3** Der 'caliver' war zwar schwächer als der 'hackbut', hatte aber den Vorteil eines Standard-Kalibers (daher der Name) und konnte in grossen Mengen an Angehörige der Miliz ausgegeben werden. **E4** Es gab nicht genug Waffen für alle eingezogenen Angehörigen der Bürgerwehr, daher wurden viele zur Verstärkung in bedrohten Gebieten als Pioniere eingesetzt.

F Veteranen der englischen Feldzüge in den Niederlanden, nach Zeichnungen von De Gheyn.

G, H Diese Figuren basieren auf Stichen von englischen Soldaten in Irland, 1587 in Derricks 'Image of Ireland' veröffentlicht. **G1** Er trägt ein 'morion', eine 'jack' und sogenannte 'venezianische' Kniehosen sowie einen linkshändigen 'caliver' (wie alle 'calivermen' in Derricks Bildern). **G2** Volle Rüstung ohne 'tassets'; die Kniehosen sind sogenannte 'trunk hose with canions', ein Rang- oder Statussymbol. **G3** Offiziere trugen keine Mäntel in Uniformfarben, selbst wenn diese an ihre Untergebenen ausgegeben wurden.

H1 Der flache Hut ist recht altmodisch, und dieser niedere Offizier kann sich ausser der 'gorget' vielleicht keine anderen Waffen leisten. Die Fahne zeigt eine Tudor-Rose in jeder Ecke des Kreuzes. **H2** Man beachte die 'peascod'-Jacke und die 'trunk hose with canions' mit Hosenlatz. **H3** Wilde Grenzsoldaten aus dem schottisch-englischen Grenzgebiet, beritten, mit Kettenhemden, Speeren, kleinen Schilden und eigenen Waffen.

I1 Die grobe Wollmütze, der lange Mantel und die grossen Kniehosen finden sich in allen der wenigen zeitgenössischen Bilder von Seeleuten; dieses stammt aus 'The Mariners Mirror' von 1588. **I2** Der höhere Status des geschickten Gewehrschützen ist an seinem Kostüm zu erkennen. Man beachte wieder die weiten Kniehosen. Er hält ein Zündholz, um das Gewehr mit einer Lunte zu feuern. **I3** Nach einem Porträt von Kapitän Martin Frobisher, ein kriegslustiger Zeitgenosse von Francis Drake.

J1 Ebenso wie die folgenden Tafeln nach den Werken Theodor de Breys und zeitgenössischen Stichen. **J2** Die flandrische Armee war ein ziemlich wilder Haufen, unbezahlt und deshalb gezwungen, sich aufs Plündern zu verlegen. **J3** Die Pikenträger eines 'tercio' waren in schwere, bewaffnete und leichte, unbewaffnete Männer unterteilt. Dieser Krieger diente bei dem sogenannten 'Dandy-Tercio' und ist üppig gekleidet.

K1 Dieser leichte Pikenträger diente bei dem dunkel gekleideten 'Sextons-Tercio'. **K2** Das Kriegerdasein war ein ehrenvoller Beruf für den ehrgeizigen jüngeren Sohn einer Adelsfamilie; der Reichtum der Männer spiegelte sich in ihrer Ausrüstung und Bekleidung. **K3** Eine überjacke schützt das teurere Wams; er trägt einen bequemen Hut, bevor er in die Schlacht geht. Das Burgundkreuz war das Fahnenzeichen vieler spanischer Einheiten in den Niederlanden.

L1 Die spanische Kavallerie hatte modernere Feuerwaffen als die Engländer und wies daher viele dieser Krieger auf; die 'hargulatiers' verbanden die in England von den 'light horse' und 'petronels' wahrgenommenen Aufgaben der leichten Kavallerie. **L2** Die spanische schwere Kavallerie war durch einen Mangel an passenden Pferden eingeschränkt. Der 'Cassack'-Mantel findet sich in allen Illustrationen und wurde vielleicht während der Schlacht über der Rüstung getragen. **L3** Diese schwarz gepanzerten Pistolenschützen dienten als Söldner beim englischen, französischen, spanischen und niederländischen Heer, je nach Angebot.